CARCERATION STATE

A Struggle to Live Beyond Mistakes

JAMES KÜHNEL

PAGE PUBLISHING, INC.
New York, NY

First originally published by Page Publishing, Inc. 2018

ISBN 978-1-64298-326-5 (Paperback)
ISBN 978-1-64298-327-2 (Digital)

Printed in the United States of America

Ethan and Evan
"You are not forgotten"

I dedicate this book to all children whose parents are incarcerated, your voices will be heard.

"To work effectively, it is important that society's criminal process 'satisfy the appearance of justice' . . .and the appearance of justice can best be provided by allowing people to observe it."

—Warren E. Burger

ACKNOWLEDGMENTS

Mark Cornelison

Richard Adam

Axyn Prow

My wife Michelle

My mother Sandy

"I Love You Mom"

And all the others

INTRODUCTION

"There is a point beyond which even justice
becomes unjust."
—Sophocles, Electra, c. 409 BC

W here else but America, jails and prisons are business for profit?
It robs from every American, particularly tax payers, minorities,
the poor and our nations children. Yup, my dumb-ass knows this fact
all too well; I am now the property of one of America's *Department of
Corrections* (DOC). I am no longer recognized as a person, no longer
have the right to vote (though I hope to regain that right someday)
or carry arms. I am now simply a number, my new sole purpose,
generate revenue for a carceration state, known as Idaho.

This here is a note of warning. America is traveling on a rutted
road heading in the wrong direction, leaving many scars, ruining
lives, and most all, destroying American families. This warning is
to make all aware that our American justice system is being run as
a business for profit, not just privately run prisons (prison for profit
such as Correctional Corporations of America) but state-run facilities as well. Our justice system is outdated and out of control. It is
an abuse of authority, exploiting citizens to harsh, cruel, and often
extreme punishments to keep its wheels turning for profit. This dangerous path is jeopardizing our economy and putting your children's
future and America's future in a difficult position for many generations to come.

I will bring forth all I have experienced and witnessed. My hope is that you come away with a better understanding of how your justice system works, and why it doesn't work. America's vile system is truly dishonest, untrustworthy, unprincipled, and fraudulent in so many ways. It is manipulative, hurtful, immoral, ineffective, evil, dysfunctional, and full of corruption! Yes I'm saying America's so-called justice system, especially Idaho's, is sick with a bad case of corruption and infested with greed. Sadly I don't see any cure in sight.

My hope is that you come to understand why America has the highest incarceration rate in the world (America has more people locked up than China, a nation with ten times our population). And why many states as well as federal penitentiaries are maxed out, full beyond capacity, and why many states are turning to the privately run prison industry, housing their inmates outside their borders. I will expose all I have come to know about Idaho's so-called justice system from its county jails to its prison system, as well as its probation and parole department. I will also share my own experience with Idaho's Department of Corrections treatment programs (the few available) so you will understand why IDOC treatment programs continue to fail you, the American taxpayer. You will also come to understand how and why our justice system continues to fail its citizens by creating monsters who become criminals for life. Referring to one of her many spells of imprisonment, US temperance campaigner, Carry Nation (1846–1911) wrote, "You have put me in here a cub, but I will come out roaring like a lion, and I will make all hell howl!"

I will open doors and reveal America's justice, its dark side, its true colors. Sadly my friends they are not barred and striped in red, white, or blue. I will bring forth the truth and give facts for all to see and recognize that America (and states like Idaho) have built its justice system to profit lawmakers and their well-to-do friends, all off the backs of the very citizens they were elected by and are supposed to be working for, incarcerating those very citizens at the expense of taxpayers and America's youth. Lady Justice, she walked out of Idaho and America a very long time ago. Now it is time *We The People* help bring Lady Justice back and save our communities, our citizens from the harsh reality of what Idaho and American justice has created for profit.

Please don't take what I'm saying the wrong way—hear me out. Jails and prisons are absolutely needed. Justice is needed, but prison for profit is just wrong and has nothing to do with justice. American lawmakers should be ashamed of themselves for ignoring Lady Justice for profit, for locking up your children to line their own pockets while they and their children walk away from crimes you or your children could never walk away from.

I do not claim innocence nor do I claim to be a victim. I am simply a man who made mistakes and trying to live beyond them. My belief is, if you break a law, you deserve to be punished within reasonable fairness of said law broken. No one is above the law, including public officials, politicians, or the wealthy. Not me, not you (sorry to say), not anyone—laws must be respected and enforced, within fairness and reason. And it's not OK to break a law to enforce a law. Unfortunately, this is often the case here in America (the police killings of unarmed black men as well as poor white men in the very communities they were sworn to protect) and the ones in power who do infringe on your rights, breaking these laws in blind attempts to enforce them and hide behind the law, untouched.

I will also bring forth my own involvement (my part) with the justice system (particularly Idaho's, since that is where I have been imprisoned) from start to finish, exposing myself and my humility, the shame I have come to know from being raped, beaten, and robbed while serving my time, my punishment. I will share what it is like being locked in a cage as an animal for years, the havoc that plays on one's mind, body, and spirit, the endless hours of torment, depression, insomnia, and loneliness, the want to end it all, to take my own life (literally) and be free from my torment and anguish.

Though I fear retaliation (as I wait to go in front of the parole commission here in Idaho, again) the dark side of America's justice system must be told. Any incarceration for profit is wrong, it is a crime against humanity, and it is unacceptable! I am standing up and speaking out for what I feel is the right thing to do. I am holding American lawmakers accountable for infringing on the constitutional and civil rights of American citizens. I am questioning both politicians and lawmakers' competence and integrity. America deserves effective, intelligent leaders working for their constituents, not just for the rich, the good ol' boys, the select few. Not for themselves, to line their pockets or that of their family and friends, but for all Americans. I believe it is time America's leadership starts earning their pay, stop wasting tax dollars, and do something right for the American public.

My goal is to awaken your sense of curiosity, inform you, and leave you wanting to know and do more (like vote responsible men and women into office). You will draw your own logical, sensible conclusion, and I pray you will become proactive for a better America today.

With each page and every chapter, you will come away with a better understanding of the justice system, its dark side and true colors, and you will see and feel what I have experienced while behind prison walls. I will share my journey into the internal fires of Hades, my humility, so all can learn from my mistakes and experiences. Please consider what I am saying, America is out of control. Life is too short. America will lock away your children and your future to profit a select few, to ensure re-elections and line pockets, calling it justice. Welcome, my friends, to my story, my life. Welcome to the dark side of American politics and prison for profit.

CHAPTER 1

President Obama

The number of state and federal prisoners in the United States more than tripled during President Ronald Reagan's and George H. Bush's (Republicans) tenure and continued to steadily climb under President Bill Clinton's (Democrat) term. Quadrupling during the 1980s and 1990s, increasing from about 319,000 in 1980 to 773,000 in 1990 and 1,302,000 in 1999, and by the year 2016, 2.3 million. And another half million plus are in county jails throughout the country at any given time. More than one in every 150 people in the United States is in prison or jail. Idaho's numbers are even higher than the national average. Individuals convicted of drug offenses constitute the largest group of inmates in the United States, representing nearly sixty percent of all federal prisoners and twenty-one percent of all state prisoners, Idaho's drug related prison population is even higher than the national average.

Millions of criminal records (nearly one-fifth of the entire US population) are stuffed into police files. Hundreds of billions of dollars have poured from taxpayers' checking accounts into penal institutions and the businesses that service them. Several million people have come to depend on the criminal justice system for employment.

The hidden side of the growth of the criminal justice system is its direct effect on how much less money Americans spend on education, parks, libraries, recreation centers, highways, and universities. With a significant percentage of the potential male work force in prison, our high rates of incarceration also act as a drag on economic growth.

Most male prisoners in the United States are poor and members of minority groups. African-Americans make up 14 percent of the nation's population and yet they comprise 36 percent of the prison population. Hispanics comprise about 18 percent of the male inmate population.

Nearly 94 percent of all prisoners in state and federal US prisons are male. However, because of stricter drug laws passed in the Nixon, Reagan, Bush, and Clinton years, since 1990, the annual growth of the female inmate population in federal and state prisons has been 8.8 percent per year, compared with an annual growth rate of male offenders of 6.9 percent. In 1998, female inmates accounted for 6.5 percent of all prisoners nationwide, up from 5.7 percent in 1990. According to the sentencing report, in 2010, black women were incarcerated at nearly three times the rate of white women (733 versus 47 per 100,000), while Hispanic women were incarcerated at 1.6 times the rate of white women.

The exploding prison population in the United States has turned the heads of lawmakers and citizens alike. Is this tougher stance on sentencing really benefiting society? Is increasing the prison population in the United States to an all-time high really effective? Does convicting criminals at higher rates with longer sentences really keep America safe? Does the threat of imprisonment deter potential criminals? Do prisons rehabilitate criminals? One would think the extraordinary expansion of the criminal justice system would have made at least a small dent in the crime rate. Yet the National Criminal Justice Commission argues that imprisonment is not effective, that the increase in the prison population did not reduce crime, nor did it make Americans feel safer. In fact, some criminologists have argued that the overuse of the penal system for so many small-time offenders has actually created more crime than it has prevented.

In a 1996 publication, the National Criminal Justice Commission argues that the prison system wastes public resources, converts non-violent offenders into violent criminals, and disproportionately punishes some racial groups. Sending such a high number of Americans through the jailhouse door each year has wide ramifications. Anyone who has been handcuffed by police knows how deeply humiliating the experience can be. Imagine the effects of spending even a night in the bizarre and violent subculture of most jails. Literature abounds with examples of people traumatized by the experience. Each person booked is fingerprinted and photographed for their criminal record (the record remains with them even if the charges are later dropped). Basic survival tactics are necessary to endure even a short stay. Inmates learn to strike first and seek strength in gangs often comprised of dangerous offenders. Sexual assaults are frequent and usually go unpunished. As more young men and women are socialized to the cell blocks and then are returned to the streets, the violent subculture of the correctional facility increasingly acts as a vector for crime in our communities. Prisons and jails thus have a dual effect: they protect society from criminals, but they also contribute to crime by transferring their violent subculture to our community once inmates are released. I believe former President Obama agrees with the National Criminal Justice Commission's findings.

President Barack Obama addressed America's prison problem in his 2014 State of Union Address, straightforwardly mentioning several states, including Idaho as having a notoriously inflated prison populations. Obviously, if the president of the United States recognizes America's prison problem and he addresses and even references Idaho during his State of the Union Address, it must be something much more than I, or the American public, knows of.

President Obama later met with a group of federal inmates (the only president to visit a prison in the history of the United States), afterwards using his executive power passing laws to release more than five thousand nonviolent federal inmates sentenced under harsh federal mandatory minimum sentencing act. He also revamped the federal Three Strikes Law, changing the mandatory life sentencing to a maximum of twenty-five years for prisoners convicted of three federal crimes. Many states have failed to follow suit (such as Idaho), and continue to give life sentences for nonviolent crimes under the Persistent Violator, or the Habitual Criminal laws.

OK, the proof is in the pudding, my friend. President Obama confirms what I'm saying to be true. He and the federal government both recognize that there is a serious problem with the American justice system and its accompanying prison system, especially here in Idaho. The million-dollar question is, what are those problems, and how do we—you and I—help to fix them?

As you read on, you will come to understand what some of the problems are, and yes, I'm saying it's much more than it appears. It is not just a prison problem; this is an American problem. This is a problem that affects all Americans, especially the poor. This is a problem that separates classes, a way to ensure the wealthy stay in power and increase their wealth while stripping the poor of their rights, of the American Dream. As you read on, my hope is that you will want to become proactive and stand up and help solve these threatening problems. By doing so, you could save our country from this tyranny. The life you save could be your own, your sons' or daughters', your families', possibly even America's future.

CHAPTER 2

I'm More Than a Number

When sentenced to prison, you are given a number. This number is your prison identification, declaring and recognizing you as state property. Your identity becomes that number. For me, once I had become that number, I lost myself, and my self-worth. It became a mind game, telling me I was nothing, stripping me of my identity. I was no longer James; I was merely 94032.

Bull-crap! I refuse to be known as a number, any longer. I'm James; I feel and bleed just like any other man in this world. I'm a person who has a strong belief in God and I love all animals. And I'm a big sports fan; Thanksgiving is my favorite holiday. I have a green thumb and a knack for growing roses I have a passion for cooking, and I truly love being in and around water, I love to surf. I have worth, and I am more than a number! I am a human being, just like you; the only difference is I have a prison number on my back. This number almost killed me. This number is not who I am. With this book, I am taking my life back and I'm giving that number back to Idaho so that they can put it where the *sun don't shine*, right up their ass, hope it hurts; then again, the truth usually does. What I'm saying is the pen is mightier than any sword!

Hello, my name is James, and yes, I am more than a number. I am a husband, a father, and a son. I am also your neighbor and a co-worker. I shop in the same stores as you. I am so much more, but most of all, I am James. For so many years, I had let my state-issued number control my identity (no more). It took away who I was, simply because I made a mistake and was sentenced to prison. Yes, I've made mistakes in my life, and I am paying the price for them. I am very sorry for all the taxpayers who are paying my bill while I am serving my debt to society. However, I cannot allow a number to hinder my identity any longer. I would become worthless to my family, to all, including myself if I do. I'm done crying, my friend. I deserve better, and so do you.

I know I'm a good person, and because of my experience with our American justice system, I must give back, explain, teach and help. In return, I will help myself. Hey, it's a win-win for all who care to listen and learn from my experiences and mistakes, so you do not become a number like me. I'm happy to say James is back and here to help.

It is not just me carrying the burden of a state-issued number. Between the years of 2003–2009, over twenty-one thousand people in Idaho (where I am imprisoned), became a prison number. Between the years of 2009–2016, another thirty-one thousand people received a prison number. In fifteen years, fifty-two thousand Idaho citizens had become a source of income for the *careration state*, a state with a population of less than one and a half million people.

CHAPTER 3

The Beginning of a Nightmare

M y nightmare began at the age of thirty-nine, when I received my Idaho prison number. I was arrested for a felony domestic battery and felony attempted strangulation. Domestic battery is considered a misdemeanor unless there is bodily harm or threat of death. Though I am not defending my behavior, please remember there are two sides to every story.

My girlfriend (at the time) and I began arguing about some money missing from my wallet. I became heated when she denied taking the money, though it was obvious she had taken it, she was the only one that could have. The more she denied it, the more enraged I became, and I began throwing things around (my bad). The only physical altercation during our argument was initiated by her attempts to stop me from throwing things, especially her things. I assure you, I never raised a hand to her, nor was it my intent to harm her in any way. However, she did obtain a small cut on her right thumb due to a window I broke (accidentally) when she was picking up some of her belongings off from the ground. At some point, during our argument I went outside to gather my thoughts and to cool down. While I was walking around the front yard, out of anger

I kicked a small flower pot that was on the ground. I dam near broke my foot, turned out this flower pot was frozen solid.

Hurting my foot just fueled my anger. Yes, I got mad, and I picked up that flower pot, and I was going to smash it on the ground, so I thought.

As I said, it was frozen solid. Thus, it was much heavier than I expected it to be. As I went to throw it forward, to the front of me it veered off to the right of me, striking the roof of my mother's truck.

My god, if it wasn't for dumb luck, I wouldn't have any luck at all. As I stood there watching this flower pot smash the passenger roof area, it paused there for a moment before it rolled over on the passenger side window, breaking it (not my finest hour). When the police finally showed up hours later and found dried blood on her right thumb area. I was done off to jail I went, though it was an accident and no medical attention was needed for the cut, and this was my first arrest in the state of Idaho. I was given the maximum sentence of eight years in prison, and off to prison I went.

My second prison sentence was given in the same state. I was out of prison and on parole when I met a woman, Michelle, and started dating. About three months into our relationship, I was talking to my parole officer (PO) about my new girlfriend, this was not good. My parole officer demanded I end this relationship immediately, informing me that entering into relationships was a violation of my parole. I was devastated and confused; I was in love and had no idea what to say or do.

A few months later, my housing lease was ending at the end of the month, and I wasn't sure if I wanted to stay or find somewhere else to live. About a week before my lease was up, the place next to my girlfriend's house came up for rent. It was a perfect location and in my price range, so I immediately put a deposit down securing the lease. Though I did not know it at the time, that this would be my down fall. My parole officer was on vacation at that time, I put in the proper paperwork informing the parole office of my new residence. My parole officer was angered by the move, but there was nothing she could do about it (so I thought). However, a few days later, my PO some how found out that I had moved next door to the women I was dating, my PO unleashed the fury of the abyss itself on me. I was called into my PO's office and told I had no business dating an older blind woman without her permission. I was immediately arrested and taken to the Ada County Jail in Boise, Idaho, for a period of six days, a punishment time to think about what I had failed to do (not following my parole). As she was booking me into the jail, I asked her to please give my truck keys to my mother so she would be able to retrieve my truck from Probation and Parole's parking lot. Earlier that day, I bought a new washer and dryer, and they were still in the back of my truck, plus I had the alarm set and my mother didn't have the remote to turn it off. My parole officer said no problem, and I happily handed her the keys to my truck, thinking this was nice of her to do this for me. An hour later, I was pulled from the holding cell I had been placed in and questioned about an empty baggie found on the passenger side of my truck, this baggie, testing positive for methamphetamine. I was shocked—I had no idea what this was about at that time—but nevertheless, I was immediately arrested for possesion of methamphetamine.

Turns out, my parole officer and her partner, went to where my truck was parked and searched my truck and allegedly found an empty baggie that tested positive for methamphetamine and a used needle, both are misdemeanors in most states. I do not deny the fact that I have self-medicated at times in my life, but never have I ever self-medicated by using a needle.

However, since I was not present during this search, and I do not recall ever having an empty baggie or a used needle in my truck. Although these items were found on the passenger side I cannot say with any certainty that these items were actually found in my truck.

Nonetheless, there was evidence being DNA that would have proven that the used needle that was allegedly found in my truck was not used by me, there for the DNA evidence would have brought doubt to the items found in my truck. Unfortunately, for me as I was waiting for DNA results to come back from a laboratory, my public defender tells me that the used needle that held DNA proof of my innocence is missing. It somehow mysteriously disappeared from evidence.

Nonetheless, without the DNA evidence I was convicted for possession of methamphetamine that was found miles from where I was. Though there was no visible, weighable or usable amount of meth in this baggie. It was just a baggie containing a residue that tested positive. Furthermore, the drug paraphernalia charge (the used needle) was dismissed, and I received the maximum sentence of seven years back to prison I went.

As for the brand new washer and dryer I bought, they were both donated to a local charity by my mother in the Boise area a few days after I was arrested.

After serving time and being released on parole again, I married Michelle, the woman I was dating. She waited for me all those years. My wife, Michelle, is legally blind; it is what it is. I love my wife very much, and I will stand by her no matter what, as she did for me while I was in the abyss of my life in prison. Life with little sight is not easy for my wife, I do what I can to help her, I do what I can to make her life as best as I can. However, I was not aware at the time we married of all the other disabilities my beautiful wife struggles with like, ADHD, bipolar and personality disorders. Meaning she has three totally different personalities living inside her head. Two of them constantly wanting to come out to play, making my life miserable.

One of them is my loving wife Michelle, whom is sane and rational, when on her meds. Another is a slut named Monika, and the third is their evil twin, a she-devil from the deepest reaches of Hades.

And if that is not enough, then there are the female hormone issues. Trust me, it's a struggle and a nightmare trying to keep all of this in balance. Nevertheless, as I have said, I love my wife very much and I have come to understand how important medication is to her mental stability (as to mine). Unfortunately, my dumb ass like everything else learned this the hard way. My wife is far from being perfect, then again neither am I.

We both accept each other for who we are, and the love we share when in perfect balance, it really is amazing and that's worth fighting for.

Not realizing my wife's imbalances at that time, I had no clue she had been off her medication for several days (my bad). There was no reasoning with her while in this state; there was no talking to her. I was overwhelmed and to the point of being broken by my wifes, verbal abuse. I was honestly frightened; I knew another domestic battery charge could send me back to prison for life under Idaho's *Persistent Violator Enhancement laws*. I was confused; I had enough of my wife's behavior and mental breakdowns and decided I had to leave. As I was packing my things, all the fires of the underworld broke loose when Michelle realized I was leaving, and I was forced to leave without anything I was trying to pack.

Not having my wallet or any money, I had no choice but to call my mother for help. During our conversation, I explained to my mother what was going on with Michelle, we both agreed it would be best if someone was there to help keep the peace while collecting some of my things, to keep it from becoming a nightmare. I went to the Boise Police Department asking for help. When I got there, I was told there was no one there that could help me, and that I should bring a third person along to assist me if I planned on going back home. Shocked by this, I sat down in the Boise Police Department's waiting room feeling hopeless and wondering what to do. Shortly after, two Boise police officers walk up asking if I was James. I excitedly replied that I was thinking I was about to get the help I had been seeking but found myself immediately detained and questioned. Less than five minutes later, I was arrested for domestic battery (misdemeanor) and tampering with a communication devise (a felony). Just my luck, I'm going back to prison for something I didn't do.

As I was being booked into the Ada County Jail, luck found me. The booking officer informed me that the investigating officer filing the police report made an error and that the felony charge of tampering with a phone was actually a misdemeanor. I was now being charged with two misdemeanors, thinking this would not send me back to prison (thank the Lord). This being on a Friday, I sat in the Ada County jail waiting to go to my arraignment on Monday. Unfortunately during my arraignment, luck was not there (gone to lunch), it went bad real quick! Because of my first domestic battery many years back, this misdemeanor was automatically amended to a first-rate hardcore felony (just my luck).

So here I am, back in the Ada county jail, facing another domestic battery (felony) and tampering with a phone (misdemeanor). Also, during my arraignment, a no-contact order was filed by the district attorney (without my wife's permission and against her will). This meant no contact with Michelle whatsoever. To make a long story short, the end results were as follows: domestic battery (felony) dropped/dismissed, tampering with a phone (misdemeanor) dropped/dismissed (though both charges were dismissed, they both remain on my record). Now you would say this was good, right? Nope, my dumb ass called home to my wife seven times after the no-contact order was put in place. I broke the no-contact order. So back to prison I shall go. New charges were filed by the district attorney, and I had no choice but to accept the plea deal I was given or face a possible life sentence under Idaho's Persistent Violator Enhancement Charge.

It was all coming to a head so quickly, I was now being charged with two misdemeanors and one felony violating a no-contact order (NCO) and a second felony for intimidating a state's witness. Now the intimidating of a state's witness was a bullcrap lie made up by the prosecuting attorney. The prosecuting attorney was saying I intimidated my wife to change her story when I was on the phone with my mother. The prosecuting attorney said I had used my mother by saying the words "Mom, it has to be 100 percent or I don't have a chance." Somehow, those few words turned this charge into a felony, and let's not forget that the original charges were dismissed and yet I was still charged for a crime, based on a dismissed charge. My wife, Michelle immediately came forward after I was arrested informing the prosecuting attorney that she lied out of anger, long before that phone call I had with my mother.

Furthermore, after I was arrested my wife had given a sworn confession to an investigator. My wife's statement or confession was recorded as evidence. Again, I will say, this statement or confession was recorded long before I said, "Mom it has to be 100 percent, or I don't have a chance.

Unfortunately, once again evidence in my case was lost. Somehow the recorded statement or confession my wife had given to an investigator magically disappeared from evidence.

I had no choice, but to take the plea deal I was offered by the prosecuting attorney. I was now being threatened, take a plea deal, or face a potential life sentence under Idaho's Persistent Violator Enhancement. This threat was real. I had witnessed it happen to others, and I was terrified. My court-appointed public defender was of no help, constantly telling me I had no choice, so I reluctantly took the deal, pleading guilty to two misdemeanor no-contact order violations, one felony no-contact violation, and a felony intimidating of a witness (good deal right).

During my sentencing, I stood in front of a judge and lied. I had no choice; I was forced to lie when my life, my freedom, and my future was at risk. I had to say I did things I did not do; I was being threatened by the prosecuting attorney. It was either say it or face life. My public defender and the prosecuting attorney forced my hand. This was wrong, and it is what it is, my friend. There is no place for right or wrong, no place for guilt or innocence, nor even truth in justice. I was sentenced to another eight years in prison.

Being arrested started a domino effect of many bad situations in my life. I was jailed then imprisoned. I have lost everything I had worked my entire life for, lost it all. After my first arrest, my ex-girlfriend, the one with the cut thumb, robbed me, took everything from a storage locker I had rented. For years, while I was in prison, I was paying for a storage locker that was empty. She left a note on the wall saying "LOL" with a smiley face. She took everything I owned and the kitchen sink. In recent times, I got word that she is now holding my family's photos, photos of my kids for ransom. For years she pretended to be my wife when I was in prison and ruined my credit by using my social security number. She even had a few credit cards of mine, which I had no clue of. Though she is a preacher's daughter, this woman is truly evil. God have mercy to all who come her way.

Becoming a felon has changed my life; it changed everything. Due to my record, I'm now recognized as being a violent drug user. Doors that were open are now closed. My life will never be the same.

I'm forever on the edge of society, looking down at suicide (This scares the hell out of me). The price of being a felon could never be paid, even after paying one's debt to society. This was the beginning of a lifelong nightmare, and there is no end in sight when becoming a felon in America, especially in states like Idaho. People with felony conviction cannot get food stamps in many states or qualify for TAMF. Many local housing authorities bar people with drug convictions. The job market is even more of a hustle territory; felony convictions instantly close the door of opportunity.

One of every twenty-five adults males living in Idaho are in prison or on parole. The numbers are higher for those convicted of felonies and have been released from probation, prison, or parole. Though Idaho felons do regain their voting rights, the state confuses and frustrates released felons to the point of not caring, and not voting. Idaho also claims to be a state of outdoor life, but felons are stripped of their hunting rights and many are discouraged (by probation and parole officers) from weekend camping or fishing trips. Sadly, in today's America, felons are being discriminated against and there are no laws to stop this type of discrimination.

CHAPTER 4

Kangaroo Court

A mother of a friend said, "I used to think police, judges, and courts were like the old Mickey Rooney films, that they were out to help everyone, do what's right, what's best for everyone. But after seeing what Idaho has done to my son, it's worse than having your dreams crushed." America's justice system is nothing like what is seen on television. Judges have become useless symbols of what justice used to be. District attorneys are the judges, juries, and the executioners. Judges are merely puppets, controlled by politicians and district attorneys. In other words, judges work so closely with politicians and district attorneys, that judges themselves act as if they too are a district attorney or a lawmaker (instead of law interpreter). They no longer interpret the law but act as district attorneys, wanting only convictions, caring little of guilt or innocence, of right or wrong, rubber-stamping their way to re-elections at the expense of the taxpayer. And yes, rubber-stamping is a form of corruption.

America is the greatest country in the world. I'm proud to be an American, and I would give my life without question to protect it and our rights. I am proud and grateful for every man and woman that has worn a United States uniform, especially those who have made that ultimate sacrifice, to each and every one of them, God bless them and their families. These men and women are national treasures; they gave their lives to defend our freedom and civil rights. But I am sure, most—if not all—would be embarrassed by today's America, if they knew the real truth. I know I am.

Idaho has a huge population of war veterans incarcerated, most of which suffer mental health disorders such as post-traumatic stress disorder (PTSD). A large number suffering from such disorders have been imprisoned for self-medicating (drug use). Instead of offering our war heroes the help they deserve, they are incarcerated for injuries inflicted while serving our country. I am embarrassed by states like Idaho, in how they treat their citizens, especially their veterans, for what I believe is incarceration for profit, at the expense of the very taxpayer they are supposed to be protecting. I truly believe this behavior is a complete disrespect to the men and women who gave their lives for this great country.

Incarceration is also a way of separating classes the same way the Jim Crow System separated black and white citizens in the 1870s. This system of segregation also included the denial of voting rights, known as disfranchisement, much like felons are denied the right to vote in today's system. They strip the voting rights of those who vote against them, frightening the rest with propaganda to gain their votes, much like the Nixon administration did during the early seventies.

A top aid in the Nixon administration openly admitted that Nixon's War on Drugs was a way to curve and prevent the poor (who usually vote Democrat), particularly African-Americans and the so-called *hippies* from voting. In other words, the Nixon administration imprisoned what they considered the undesirables to advance their parties agenda (the Republican Party). This disfranchisement of felons has had a great effect on our country and still continues today. More than half of the male African-American population in the state of Florida has had their voting rights stripped, most due to low-level drug offences. Florida does not reinstate voting rights.

I don't believe the people of Idaho intentionally incarcerate their veterans, their young, or their poor for profit. However, to interpret laws is almost always corrupt (Voltaire, *Philosophical Dictionary*, 1764), and when a politician can interpret laws in their favor (to profit themselves), they almost always do so. And that is exactly what Idaho lawmakers have done. They have followed the Nixon administration's lead, frightening Idaho citizens by claiming Idaho has a serious crime problem due to drugs (much like the Jim Crow advocates claimed African-Americans were a scourge to society and a threat to white America's way of life, today's lawmakers make the same claim about drug use and convicted felons). To counter this problem, states like Idaho adopted harsher, tough-on-crimes policies at the city and county level. The criminalization of poverty has led the way, often under the banner of zero tolerance. The flow of people into our county jails and prisons has been enhanced by aggressive radicalized policing largely inspired by the war on drugs and the war on immigrants, and in a very short period, both county jails and prisons became overwhelmed, filled, maxed out beyond their capacity.

Lawmakers then turned to the private prison industry, moving Correction Corporation of America (CCA) and the Management Training Corporation (MTC, also known as CAPP) into Idaho. Idaho has also used the GEO Corporation (a private prison owned by republican Vice President Dick Cheney) and other private prisons to house inmates, all of which have donated large amounts of money to Idaho Lawmaker's campaign funds, perpetuating the situation by influencing lawmakers to send Idaho inmates to other states like Minnesota, Oklahoma, Colorado, New Mexico, Texas, Arkansas, and Louisiana.

This cozy deal kept prisons and lawmakers' pockets full with cash (blood money) while stripping the rights of the poor and frightening the rest to ensure re-elections. Once Idaho learned that a profit could be made from incarceration as the behavior continued, and is still going on today. This behavior is corruption and it's criminal! And yes, it got the attention of the federal government and President Barack Obama. America is in turmoil and needs to be saved from this corruption. We, the people, deserve better from the American leadership (especially Idaho's leadership).

As I was going to court, I witness first-hand in how prosecuting attorneys operate. What I experienced was something other than justice, it was inappropriate to the point of blatant neglect and, on some levels, even criminal. The prosecuting attorney's behavior seemed more personal than professional, as if they were worried more about the conviction than about justice. When arrested, my wife, Michelle made a statement and filled out a police report. She immediately came forward recanting her statement, confessing to the prosecuting attorney that she had lied in a moment of anger. However, the prosecuting attorney, the same one that sent me to prison on my first domestic battery, refused to hear, accept, or believe my wife's confession. Though my arrest was based solely on my wife's statement (there was no other witness or other evidence what so ever), the prosecuting attorneys refused to hear any further statements.

Soon after my wife retracted her statement, confessing that her declarations were in retaliation for my leaving her, the prosecuting attorney stopped returning my wife's phone calls, even refusing to talk to her before and after any of my court appearances. This behavior was very disrespectful considering that she, my wife was being called the victim in this case. It was then that Michelle and I understood the real truth. Prosecuting attorneys' only concerns are their conviction percentages—guilt and innocence, right and wrong having little or nothing to do with justice.

District and prosecuting attorneys are often lawbreakers themselves, not only willing to use illegal means to secure conviction but also blatantly defying the law with the belief they are above the very laws they are entrusted to serve. One such case involved a prominent Idaho prosecutor and libertarian gubernatorial hopeful, John Bujak. Bujak was charged with the theft of three hundred thousand dollars ($300,000 taxpayer dollars). Though he openly admitted to taking the money and using it to catch up his home payments, he was never convicted and the money never returned. It is no wonder district and prosecuting attorneys believe they can get away with anything.

District and prosecuting attorneys can and will use scare tactics, threats, and intimidation. They also prepare witnesses before giving their sworn testimonies in a court of law as they tried to do with my wife (attempting to convince her to give her original recanted statement). Dirty tricks are common play for prosecuting attorneys. They ignore the truth, the facts, and even when there is no evidence, they twist facts in attempts to create evidence from nothing. These tactics are far more than simply confined to Idaho. This is an American problem that has grown progressively worse over the years. James Garrison, a prominent district attorney in New Orleans, Louisiana, once said, "This is not the first time I have arrested somebody and then built my case afterwards."

Towards the end of my case, I was faced with the worse kind of situation, one could ever imagine. The prosecuting attorney was threating to arrest both my wife and mother if I refused to accept a plea deal. And to add a little more insurance and persuasion, prosecuting attorney filed a Habitual Offender Enhancement, a potential life sentence under President Bill Clinton's (Democrat) Three Strikes Law, enacted during his tenure in the early '90s. President Clinton has since admitted these laws were one of his biggest mistakes, and President Obama has done away with life sentences under the Federal Three Strikes Laws as they were written, but states (especially red Republican states such as Idaho) have failed to follow suit. This final act of aggression was the insurance securing my future in prison. My wife's original statement said I had pushed her to our couch (nothing more). And because of those words, words she later recanted, and all I have witnessed and experienced while attempting to defend myself in our justice system, I was made to feel like *public enemy number one.*

Since I could not afford a private attorney, a public defender was appointed by the courts. Idaho's public defenders have caseloads numbering in the hundreds, making it impossible to adequately represent anyone, though it is our constitutional right as an American citizen (the Sixth Amendment). The American Civil Liberties Union (ACLU) recently sued Idaho because of this fact, and though all admitted there was a problem, nothing was done to help fix this problem. Unfortunately the case was dismissed and this problem still continues on today. Sadly those who are using the services of a public defender's office are not getting adequate representation. Meaning they are having these constitutional rights violated specifically our 6th Amendment.

Public defenders rarely meet with their clients other than the very day of court (usually in the courtroom itself) and are always pushing their clients into plea deals that no normal person would ever accept. When someone is represented in such a way, it leads one to believe that their court-appointed public defender is actually working for the district attorney's office. Sure, they say that is ludicrous, that they are representing you to the best of their ability, but don't fool yourself. Public defenders are usually young and straight out of law school, overworked, underpaid, and badly wanting to advance to a better position (like a deputy prosecutor). And how would a public defender advance—by not making waves, by making the prosecutor's job easy for them, by pushing terrible plea deals on their clients. Yes, I am saying that America's public defenders are in the pockets of the district attorney's office for personal gain. Ninety percent of all Idaho criminal cases end in plea deals, usually at the insistence of public defenders. The dean of the University of Southern California Law Center, Dorothy Wright Wilson, stated, "It's only because we have plea bargaining that our criminal justice system is still in motion. That doesn't say much for the quality of justice."

In my three Idaho cases, I had thirteen different public defenders representing me, each as useless and worthless as the next. In my most recent case, I was appointed seven public defenders, four different judges, and one prosecuting attorney. I was told this was normal representation and course of proceeding here at the Ada county court house. After entering the court room in chains and seated, a public defender would call out names like a grade school teacher taking role. I met six of my seven public defenders this way. Nonetheless, they would go one by one down the line of inmates offering a ridicules plea deal and expecting each inmate to make a major decision in their life within the next few seconds before the judge entered the courtroom. How is a justice system like this in any way fair? How could anyone be expected to decide their fate in such a way?

To be given merely moments to decide my future is in no way fair or right. The pressure becomes too much; bad decisions are made. I have known public defenders to lie time after time to both me and my family. I even had one public defender or the public defender's office lose evidence in my case. Obviously this was not helpful to me or my case.

Property and evidence managers and technicians are often minimally trained on how to handle and store evidence and are poorly paid. The loss or improper destruction of evidence is way more common than you think. However, mere inaction, incompetence, lack of responsibility, and negligence is not sufficient for a criminal violation, and yet their irresponsibility sends people to prison.

Once, while being held in a county jail, I missed a court date because my public defender forgot to turn in a transport order to the sheriff's department, but court was held without my being present—to speed things up and make things easier on everyone, I presume.

My public defenders had refused to do as I requested, forcing me to do what they told me to do. I was coerced to waive my preliminary hearing, to take the plea bargain (*bargain* being the key word here) or be charged with *persistent offender enhancement* (a potential life sentence). After waiving my preliminary hearing, I was appointed a different public defender, one who was totally unaware of the plea bargain or goings-on of the first public defender since he had not read my discovery or was not present during initial arraignments. However, he was aware there was a plea bargain in the works but had no idea what it was. Another public defender needlessly revealed personal information about me to the district attorney's office without my consent. Without question, this truly is inadequate representation.

There is a word for our public defenders I had heard when first arrested—*public pretenders*—and that is exactly what they do, pretend. Pretending to be a friend, pretending to help. Their behavior is an act, a show to look good in front of peers while in a courtroom. The truth, they are puppets being controlled by the district attorneys, rubber stamping their way up the ladder of wealth and success at the expense of other peoples lives and of course the taxpayers' dollars. This without question is a form of deception, fraud, and corruption. The truth is that they are not doing the job the taxpayers are paying them to do. Why is this acceptable?

Obviously I have spent a lot of time in Idaho courtrooms, and I have witnessed how district attorneys abuse their power and authority, not just with me personally but with all who enter into our American court rooms. They are hard driven for convictions and are willing to twist and hide the truth, and they have become very good at terrifying the accused into making bad decisions and mistakes as I have. The prices of these mistakes are excessive and extreme and, in some cases, even cruel and unusual, and if you are poor like me—and because of this, being poor, you don't have money for adequate legal defense—you will serve a prison sentence that is longer than those equivalent anywhere else in the industrialized world of today.

In 2015 and 2016, there was a case involving a shooting at an Idaho laundromat where the accused admitted to shooting a man in the chest at point blank range, the injured man only living because the gun jammed as the accused attempted to fire another round into the fallen man; the shooter received a twenty-five-year prison sentence. That same year, another man was arrested on a drug charge, and was also sentenced to a twenty-five year prison sentence. The second man never hurt anyone, and other than the police officers that arrested him, there were no victims in his case, no one to come forward and say, "It was him, he did it." But he received the same harsh punishment as a man shooting and trying to kill another human being.

Again, that same year, another man was given a twenty-five-year prison sentence for a fourth Driving Under the Influence (DUI). Another man, sentenced almost the same day but on his fifth DUI, received a ten-year prison sentence. I am not defending the practice of drinking and driving (hell no) but neither of them had hurt anyone, and one man received the same sentence as a man shooting a person with the intent to kill them. I met a guy in prison who was convicted for a felony DUI. He admitted to me he was drunk and asleep in a car when the police found him. The messed-up thing about this: the car he was in had no engine in it. Idaho's own governor, Butch Otter, has been convicted of more than one DUI. He never served a day in jail (why is that?). Senator Mike Crapo was convicted of DUI while working for the state of Idaho in Washington, DC; he also did not serve any jail time. Then there was Mike Magee.

Idaho Representative Mike Magee was convicted of DUI after stealing and damaging a truck and boat from an Idaho golf course. No felony charges were ever filed, and he was only convicted of a misdemeanor DUI, in which no jail time was served, though there is a mandatory minimum of two days in county jail. During a televised news cast, Governor Butch Otter stated that Magee would have to go in front of the Idaho Ethics Committee (something that he or Mike Crapo never had to do). However, guess who was in charge of Idaho's Ethics Committee? If you guessed Representative Mike Magee, you would be right. He had to face the committee he was in charge of as his punishment. He later got into some trouble during some kind of protest in eastern Idaho (a protest where he was the only protester) and was later removed from office for sexual harassment.

A guy got pulled over while driving a friend's car. Boise police searched the vehicle and found an empty pill bottle that once contained marijuana, sadly this guy was arrested and then convicted for possession of marijuana. Why, because an empty pill bottle found in a car that didn't even belong to him tested positive for marijuana? He received a maximum prison sentence of seven years (Idaho has since then loosened marijuana laws in the state). Yet about that same time, an Idaho deputy sheriff (Twin Falls County), in a fit of rage, throws a handicapped toddler across a room, killing the child. That deputy sheriff was charged with a misdemeanor—child endangerment—and was sentenced to six months' work release that was to be served in a nearby fire department (a twenty-four-hour facility where he would never have to spend even a night in a jail cell). Public outrage later forced the deputy to serve his last remaining months in the Gooding County Jail, where, though he did spend his nights in a cell, was allowed to spend his days driving around with Gooding county officers (this man who worked for the system received VIP treatment and got away with murdering a child). This wasn't justice; it was free rent.

An older man accused of raping three children received a two-year suspended sentence. This rapist went home that day, possibly to rape again (destroying young children's lives). This is true madness; this wasn't even a slap on the wrist. It doesn't make any sense. Another older man (ninety-three years old) got sixty days in the county jail for a *failure to stop* at a Stop sign ticket, a ticket that was fourteen years old. This gentleman was living in an old folks' home, in a wheelchair, and was on oxygen with extreme medical issues. He had the money to pay the fine, but that was not good enough for the prosecuting attorney; apparently, the prosecuting attorney wanted his life as well. A homeless man received ninety days in the county jail at the expense of the taxpayers for an open container of beer. After talking to this gentleman, I was informed he had done it on purpose. "Just to get out of the cold for a while because he was homeless" is what he told me. Boise, Idaho has a huge homeless population within its city limits.

It seems all sentences (especially in Idaho) are maxed-out sentences, unless you are a police officer, officer of the court, public official, or public servant. The wealthy and influential walk away from crimes you or your children could never walk away from. I have talked to hundreds (possibly thousands) of people in and out of prison while doing my research for this book. Everyone I have talked to (in Idaho prisons) was given maximum sentences according to their crime guidelines. It makes no sense to me. Case in point—a jail janitor, Salvensen, was given twenty days in the Mini Cassia criminal justice center in Burley Idaho, where he had been previously employed, after accepting a plea deal. Salvensen was accused of moving a female prisoner into an out-of-camera range then touching her sexually. Cassia County magistrate judge and a friend of the accused imposed a sentence that included 180 days in jail with 160 suspended, a $1,000 fine, supervised probation restitution, and court cost as part of the plea bargain. Salvensen's felony charge of sexual conduct with an inmate while in custody was reduced to misdemeanor battery. You can't tell me that working for the system doesn't have its privileges. Elmore County jail sergeant (a.k.a. a sheriff deputy) T. Robinson was sentenced to five days in jail after pleading guilty to disorderly conduct for violently shoving a female prisoner who was in custody into a wall, knocking her off her feet. The assault was recorded on surveillance video. Another sheriff deputy, Mitteider, reported the incident to the jail supervisors, but his concerns about what happened went unnoticed and unanswered. Mitteider was fired shortly after, for telling the truth. The moral of this story is snitching on colleagues (other cops) will get you fired because the majority who work for the system share a general cultural norm: don't be a whistleblower. I for one salute Mr. Mitteider for doing the job that the taxpayers were paying him to do and for doing what was right. The system would be a whole lot safer and better with more people like him on the job. I say thank you, Mr. Mitteider. You are a man with integrity.

My point is, there are no consistencies in sentencing, that right and wrong or truth and justice has little or nothing to do with America's justice system anymore. The infamous Washington, DC, defense attorney, F. Lee Baily, once said, "Those who think that the information brought out in a criminal trial is the truth, the whole truth, and nothing but the truth are fools. Prosecuting or defending a case is nothing more than getting those people who will talk your side, who will say what you want said . . .I use the law to frustrate the law. But I didn't set up the ground rules."

I've spent many hours on a hard, cold bench inside courtrooms waiting my turn to see a judge. Many times as I waited during recess, while the judge was off the bench, I overheard court staff talk down about their co-workers and even judges, belittling them. The behavior I witnessed was unprofessional and disrespectful, showing no filter or any fear whatsoever in what was said in front of me.

Coming and going from the county jail and courthouses is brutal. Before you leave the jail, you are securely restrained. Both ankles are shackled with a foot-long chain running from one leg to the other, and then belly chains are placed around your waist with your hands cuffed securely at your sides, limiting both your arm and foot movements. Depending on the number of court appearances to be heard, you could be chained like an animal anywhere from five to ten hours. In this amount of time, your wrist and ankles are bruised and sometimes even bleeding. Don't bother asking for medical attention. I was told on many occasions to suck it up, deal with it, and if you don't like it, then you shouldn't have come to jail. I have also spent many summer hours on a sweltering transport bus, sweating and on the verge of heat exhaustion or freezing my tail off for hours in the winter, screaming and yelling for mercy, but it does no good and, in fact, only makes it worse.

One time, during a transport from a county jail to the courthouse, a deputy sheriff acting as a transport officer was in such a hurry (to get home, I presume) that he actually sped down the highway with his car lights and sirens on, traveling at speeds in excess of

120 mph as he hummed along to a Brittney Spears CD. He thought it was funny, explaining he had to get home to watch *Dancing with the Stars*. This Ada county sheriff deputy was obviously gay by the way he was talking to me (not that their is any thing wrong with being gay) and I had the feeling he was trying to impress me (for what reason I can only imagine), but in reality, he was terrifying me and he was definitely putting my life in danger. I was not in a seatbelt (a violation of Idaho law), and all I could think of was that big-rig truck driver that I had seen early that morning who had died on the same highway due to another driver who texted while driving, cutting off the truck driver, killing him (please don't text and drive, it kills). This deputy sheriff was breaking the law, and he was scaring me, and he was putting my life in danger for his own personal needs and wants with no concern for my safety.

Another time while waiting to go to court, I was down in the courthouse's basement holding area when another inmate went to use the restroom. After entering, the bathroom door suddenly flew open as that poor man fell out and down to the ground with his pants down around his ankles, toilet paper still held in his hand. His shackles were not removed before using the restroom, and he fell while trying to wipe himself. As everyone who witnessed this were laughing, I sat there in disbelief watching the nine deputy sheriffs laughing as well, and not one of those sheriff deputies offered to help. They all were unwilling to help this man up as he struggled to stand with his pants around his ankles. Is everything in this world we live in today a joke at the expense of other human beings? Has empathy and compassion been lost and forgotten, while only shortcomings are seen?

Sure, I could go on and on forever talking about what I've seen and witnessed while being run through the American justice system and in Idaho courtrooms. But don't take my word for it. Become *proactive*—go to your own local courthouse and watch and learn. You will be appalled by the meat grinder called the American justice system. You will see the truth, the madness of how your state is abusing its power and authority over its citizens at your expense.

Obviously, it was my own my doing that put me in prison. I accept full responsibility, and I will never again disrespect or purposely violate another law or court order. I would like to end this note with one more bit of warning. If by chance you or anyone you know ends up being arrested and finds themselves in a jail cell, please, for your well-being and for your family's sake, stay off the phones while you are in any county jail. Do not become a victim of the same stupidity that I have. If you must use a phone, do not talk about your case (period) to anyone other than your lawyer. All phone calls are recorded, and trust me, district attorney offices have staff monitoring those phone calls, and they will twist your words to ensure conviction. Do not fool yourself by thinking they don't. Trust me, I went to prison because they do. What I am saying is, all phone calls from the jails are being monitored and recorded, and if district attorneys have even a slim chance of adding another conviction to their record, they can and will use anything said against you in a court of law. Please stay off the phones—your freedom, your life may depend on it. Use common sense; use your head. *Think*, especially about everything you say. Be smarter than I was. (Don't be a dumb ass.)

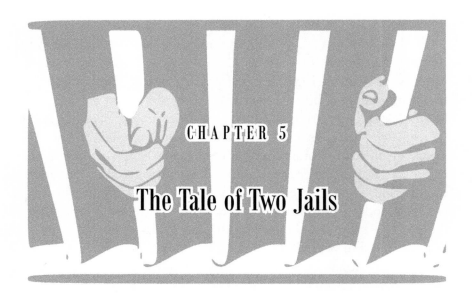

CHAPTER 5

The Tale of Two Jails

There are well over a half a million people in county jails around the United States at any given time. These county jails are distinctly different than prisons, often located in aging buildings, with very dirty and hostile environments. Jails are facilities operated by local authorities (usually county sheriffs, though most states do have local city jails operated by city police departments) and are used to confine adult criminal offenders who receive short-term sentences (in the United States, sentences of less than one year). In addition, jails are used to temporarily house individuals awaiting trial, offenders charged with crimes in other jurisdictions, probation and parole violators, and juveniles awaiting transfer to juvenile facilities.

Jails also differ from prisons in ways besides the duration of confinement. Prisons have a distinctive inmate culture and jargon, whereas most jail populations constantly change due to turnover among jail inmates, often creating a distinctly different culture. Such a turnover would lead one to believe that little opportunity exists for jail inmates to develop a prison-type culture that is perpetuated over time. However, jails frequently hold inmates that have been in and out of prison, and those inmates regularly try to instill a prison mentality among others. Gang enlistment frequently begins at the jailhouse level, and new gang recruits are required to *put in work,* to prove their loyalty, and are often asked to beat and or rob other inmates, thus causing jails to be aggressive and antagonistic environments.

Because prisons house long-term offenders, they frequently offer low-paying jobs (ranging from ten cents up to a dollar an hour) and some educational programs for inmates (not nearly enough). Most jails do not have such programs. Jails also lack other inmate amenities that exist in prisons, such as exercise facilities, commissary stores (especially where property such as televisions and clothing are sold), physicians, counselors, and other professional staff who treat or assist inmates in mental health or in other ways.

The majority of jails in the United States are small, consisting of a single building with several tiers of cells and cell blocks (horizontal groupings of cells). Prison facilities, by contrast, usually spread out over several acres, with high walls or razor-wire fences and dog runs surrounding the perimeter. Prisons are also divided into a complex arrangement of custody levels, where more dangerous inmates are separated from less dangerous ones (in Idaho, this is not always the case). In most prisons, sophisticated equipment is used to track inmate movements and promote compliance with prison rules. Armed guards occupy strategic positions in towers in an overlapping security arrangement to deter prisoners from escape attempts.

In addition, many cities and counties have also jumped on the carceration for profit bandwagon, building facilities to hold federal, state, and/or inmates from other counties and jurisdictions for profit. These jail facilities frequently compete for federal, state, and county contracts to provide revenue supporting local county jobs, usually in law enforcement, which in return fight to give out tickets or make arrests they normally wouldn't bother with (usually traffic stops and low-level drug offences), further perpetuating the incarceration cycle. I have seen inside the walls of two separate Idaho county jails, Ada and Elmore county (Boise and Mountain Home, Idaho).

My time in Elmore County was short, about seventy days. I had been sent there to do my sanction (my parole violation) after being arrested while on parole. Elmore county jail is a state holding facility for state inmates like me who are on parole. Ada county jail is not.

I have nothing bad to say about the Elmore county jail (that's the truth). The sheriff's deputies were professional, respectful, and somewhat caring. The food was palatable; I could actually identify everything I was eating. I was injured when arriving at the Elmore county jail, and their medical staff was also courteous, professional and helpful, assisting me 100 percent without it becoming a nightmare or headache. The jail itself was clean, with decent mattresses and bedding to sleep on, and not once was I ever forced to sleep on a dirty floor.

One of a few things I have found in life to be true is that people's attitudes, how they treat other human beings, is a choice. What I experienced while being held in the Elmore county jail helped open my eyes to a side of police I had never known. The sheriff's deputies who work and operate that facility chose to be professional and even caring in how they treat other human beings. I am truly grateful for this and their care during my stay there. Today, I'm saying thank you for their hospitality. However, my stay at the Ada county jail is a different tale.

During each of my three arrests in Idaho, I was transported to the Ada county jail. The Ada county jail is a large facility, holding an average between nine to twelve hundred and eighty-five detainees (inmates) at any given time. I have spent fifteen months confined within those walls, and trust me—it's nothing like Elmore county.

One of the worse things a new arrival has to endure is the initial strip search. I remember the first time a deputy sheriff stuck a finger in my rectum (a search looking for contraband). In all my time spent in and out of county jails and prison, I must have been searched over four hundred times, and I have never been touched in such a way other than the three times done by that county sheriff's department. During this search, I was suddenly surprised by the abrupt penetration of my anal cavity (this was in no way a gentle search). I jumped forward, smashing my forehead on a concrete wall, nearly knocking myself unconscious. Dazed and definitely confused by what just taken place, I became infuriated, snapping and yelling out a few choice words too profane to even write. The deputy sheriff responded by asking why I had moved. Still outraged and in a state of shock, I barked at this officer in an angered and gruff tone, asking what he thought he was doing.

Apparently, the deputy sheriff took offence to my irritable language. He turned red-faced and became hostile toward me, taking my clothing and property, leaving me naked in a cold holding cell for well over an hour (a temporary cell used while processing inmates into the jail). As I sat naked and stewing in my own humiliation, the swelling of my forehead grew to the size of a golf ball. Unfortunately for me (and my rectum), this initial search took place on three separate occasions, all by the same deputy sheriff. Each time I took that finger right up my A-hole and I said nothing. Why? Because I was afraid, humiliated, and embarrassed. After my first experience with this type of search (the finger intrusion), when realizing I had just been sexually assaulted by a deputy sheriff, I immediately felt violated and ashamed. This was the beginning of a long cycle, the first time I seriously considered the taking of my own life, the first time I longed for a life-ending bullet.

Once the booking process was complete, the finger printing, mug shot, and paperwork done, I was moved to a closed custody unit (CCU) to await classification. CCU is a very hot and extremely dirty temporary housing unit. Black mold grows in and around the shower areas and walls, and it smells like a backed-up sewer system (yes, it's that bad). Every CCU unit I have been housed in contained eight bunks, and during every one of my stays, the units were full beyond their bunk capacity and I was forced to sleep on a dirty floor among ants, stink beetles, and other various insects and trash.

CCU is supposed to be a temporary housing unit with the average length of stay being between two or three days, but people are lost and misplaced inside these units all the time. The last time I was in Ada County's CCU, I was lost in the system for nine days before it was known. On the ninth day, a classification officer happened to walk by the unit I was in. He looked questionably at me before asking, "You back again?"

"No, sir, I never left," I calmly replied.

Turns out, I was a victim of jail staff incompetence. Incompetence runs rampant throughout the Ada county jail. Why? Because there is no accountability for mistakes (the so-called *buck* is always passed). We as detainees (inmates) pay the price for their incompetence. It is the unknown price we pay for going to jail.

I also experienced video court for the first time while being held in Ada County's CCU. In all three of my video court appearances, I never once saw or talked to a judge or anyone pertaining to my case. It was over before I was able to sit down. And with all three of my cases, bail was set excessively high, making bonding out an impossible option for me. A female police officer in Oklahoma recently shot and killed an unarmed black man. She was arrested for involuntary manslaughter, and her bail was set at fifty thousand dollars. In each of my cases, my bond was no lower than one hundred thousand dollars, and I never killed anyone (I'm just saying). I have also met a man who had a one-million-dollar bond set in Twin Falls, Idaho, for a non-injury, one car DUI accident (March of 2013). Though excessive bonds are a clear violation of the eighth amendment of United States Constitution, it seems to be common practice in many states such as Idaho. High bonds help keep jail beds full, when jail beds are full the jail makes more money. This is just one example of mass incarceration for profit.

While in CCU, I witnessed people sick and violently coming down off drugs and alcohol, vomiting, suffering from dehydration, profusely sweating, putting other detainees' (inmates) lives in danger (I have seen this carnage and violence firsthand). Jail staff either ignore it (too much extra work I guess), or they simply do not care. I have seen ill and drug-crazed people passed out and wallowing in their own vomit an entire day. I have witnessed on many occasions medical emergencies that took medical and jail staff longer than twenty minutes to respond (sometimes much longer). Jail staff are inadequately trained and, in fact, they are trained to ignore detainees' medical complaints. I watched a young man who was high on something fall off a top bunk and land face down, breaking his nose. He passed out and lay face down in a pool of blood. He was completely covered in his own blood and lying unconscious by the time jail and medical staff arrived. It took staff and inmate workers days to clean the blood off the floor; his blood was everywhere. In a more recent case (August of 2016), a young man fell off his bunk at an Idaho prison and died. Though officers would not help and medical staff took more than twenty minutes to respond, inmates were threatened with disciplinary action for attempting to help (Disciplinary Order Report, or DOR), which would send an inmate to solitary confinement (the hole). Toxicology reports show drugs were involved in that 2016 case.

The reality of what I experienced and witnessed while in CCU has been mentally overwhelming for me, and I still struggle to comprehend everything I was subjected to while being held there. I was shell-shocked by the harsh treatment and loathsome sights I had witnessed to the point of developing post-traumatic stress disorder (PTSD). I couldn't understand why jail staff did little or nothing to help anyone, why they treated human beings so callously. I have always been an optimistic person, a "glass half full" type. I believed in the good of all things and people, but after my time in the Ada county jail, I felt changed. I felt I was very naïve to ever think so foolishly, to have faith and believe in mankind.

The reality of CCU was nothing compared to the true evilness that dwelled within the walls of the ADA county jail, and I was destined to see it for myself, my new home, Ada County's infamous 7-block. Officially, 7-block is a medium custody unit (MCU), but it is, in all actuality, a maximum custody unit pretending to be medium custody unit. This is fraud by deception and it is definitely a form of corruption. MCU is a twenty-two to twenty-three-hour lockdown in a cage (cell). To me and many others, it is a modern-day dungeon, a legal torture chamber, and its misery played havoc on my mind, body, and spirit. The truth is, MCU is designed (its operation) to keep detainees in a deranged state of mind by disturbing all senses. My mind, body, and spirit were under immediate and constant assault. I was a mess right from the start due to inadequate amount of rest (sleep); proper nutrition (food); clean, drinkable water; and in some cases, lack of medical attention (I was ignored when I asked for medical help on many occasions). Add stress, fear, and uncertainty into the mix, and in no time at all, mental instability and insanity take hold, inciting violence and obviously confusing, clouding, and even deranging one's decisions and judgment abilities.

Imagine trying to sleep with a fluorescent lamp glaring down above your bed twenty-four hours a day. Imaging trying to sleep when hundreds of people around you are constantly talking, yelling, even screaming for help or in some cases for mercy. Imagine trying to sleep when your cellmate is snoring like a diesel engine running poorly on five cylinders. Imagine hearing a grown man sobbing uncontrollably or, worse yet, moaning in pain and sadness all night. Imagine all this and hearing it twice as much, twice as loudly due to the reverberation of the hollow building mixed with the lonely echo of your own mind.

It is hard enough to sleep when your mind is wandering like a top wobbling at the end of its spin, but when stress and anxiety are added, it becomes overwhelming to the point of being unbearable. Imagine the fear held when your life and freedom are in the hands of people you don't know. Imagine trying to sleep when your stomach is in pain because you are hungry. Imagine trying to sleep when metal doors are constantly being slammed all day and all night long. I went days, weeks, even months without adequate amounts of rest (sleep), nutrition, and exercise. During this time, I did not understand what was going on with me or my life. I lost track of the days of the week, even forgetting what month it was at times. I became completely engulfed inside my own head and confused, lost in an abyss, in a cage, looking for sanity. I was in no condition to make any legal decisions that would affect my life, my future, or my well-being. I feel the justice system is fully aware of this fact and took advantage of not just me but others while in such a deranged state of mind.

MCU is always in a constant state of lockdown. There are sixty-three four-man cells and one six-man cell with a max capacity of two hundred and fifty-four detainees. There is what is called the *side shoot* (aka the hole), a solitary confinement unit that has eight individual cells. It is estimated that more than eighty thousand prisoners are held in some form of solitary confinement in the United States. There are no windows in MCU. Each cell has one sink/toilet combo, a single writing table, and two sets of upper and lower bunks. The recycled air is dusty and it smells. The water coming from the sink directly above the toilet is gray in color and smells as if came directly from the toilet bowl itself. And this is the only liquid available to you while incarcerated in MCU (I can only speak for myself, but this water made me sick) and it tasted awful. The water was also extremely hard and severely dried out my skin (especially my feet), causing medical problems.

There is no privacy while in MCU, especially when taking a shower. Sheriff's deputies, oftentimes female sheriff's deputies, watch inmates come and go and sometimes even while showering. This made me feel very uncomfortable, adding to my mental instability. I do admit a majority of the guys didn't care, but I did, which made me feel even more out of place. In these cells, you sleep two feet from a shared toilet that all defecate in, and believe me, your bunkies (cell-mates) are not shitting out roses. And to add to that convenience, the toilet only flushes once every five minutes (it can take me up to twenty minutes to do my business), making life in a cell a very unpleasant-smelling adventure. And let's not forget the flushing of a toilet by your head in the middle of the night; try sleeping through that. To this day, I can still hear the flushing of a toilet in my dreams.

Living in MCU while going to court is a very difficult situation. I felt my hands were tied (not literately). I was given a small window of opportunity to access phones, call home, or try to find legal assistance. Most days I was not able to use a phone due to the fact that jail staff would simply not allow me the privilege. Trying to reach any of my public pretenders (public defenders) was an impossible feat; my only option was to leave a message. The truth is, you can leave messages all day long every day, but it does no good, so don't expect a phone call back because it doesn't work that way, not in Ada County anyway.

I once received a letter by mail from my public defender requesting (at his request) a set scheduled time for me to call him. I presented this letter to a jail staff member who refused the request. I was in total disbelief. How could they deny me use of a phone at a public defender's (my lawyer) request? This is one of many ways the

American justice system abuses its power, its authority, by limiting your ability to communicate while in their custody. Because of this situation, I was not able to communicate with my attorney before my next court date. My lawyer had to request a continuance so we could talk, therefore extending my time in MCU and prolonging my situation for another month at the expense of taxpayers.

The environment I was forced to live in while in MCU changed my life (and not in a good or healthy way). I have seen more than my share of violence inside those cages, witnessing young men as they were mercilessly raped, beaten, and robbed. People are dying in there. The lucky ones die spiritually (internally); the not so fortunate die literally by means of negligence by jail staff who are not doing the job that they were hired to do. When a human being dies due to another human being negligent, it's murder! (Is it not?) Think about this—how you would feel if someone you loved died while in custody of a jail or prison due to another person's neglect or laziness, not doing the job that they were hired to do? No one should be dying, period, while in custody.

During my stay in MCU, I have had many, many different cell-mates and bunkies. One new cellmate, an older disabled man, came into MCU lost and confused like all others that had never been there before. Though he had lost his leg in some type of military accident, he was put into an upper bunk. Because of his disabilities, I offered to give up my lower bunk. That next day, the two of us approached staff to address the situation and request a bunk swap, only to be denied. Several days later, jail staff came into our cell and confiscated his artificial leg, saying it was a weapon. A few days afterwards, they gave him a single crutch to use. That crutch was more of a weapon than his artificial leg! He did get his leg back weeks later after a long battle with jail staff. This gentleman had lost his leg serving this country, protecting the rights of the very officers that were treating him so disrespectfully, and yet it was I who felt the embarrassment of his mistreatment. What I witnessed was wrong on many levels.

While in that animal cage, MCU, I had many, many first-time experiences. One such experience was with my own evil thoughts of death. All that time spent in my own head, staring out at nothing but air, hour after hour, day after day, week after week, month after month played havoc on my mind, body, and spirit. I was seeing things, weird things. My thoughts were of one thing: a mind-numbing and pain-ending bullet. Paradoxically, those same disturbing thoughts also kept me alive. It was the thought of pulling that trigger in a way for all to see, for all to know my pain, ending this nightmare, and freeing myself of the hell dwelling within my own mind. Every night I prayed to God for that bullet. Though I am still struggling with that bullet to this very day, I am so very grateful that God did not answer my prayers. I remind myself with each new day, saying, "Not today, my friend, not today."

I would like to end this note on MCU with a heads up. Do not trust the trustees (inmate workers) who wear red shirts. They are the jail house snitches and the cop's brown-nose bitches. And if by chance you are destined to see the inside and end up wearing orange-and-white striped clothing and are between the age of eighteen and twenty-seven, when you hear the yelling and screaming coming from the cages (cells), "Bring me the boy," this commotion is about one thing: you, for their entertainment and play. Be very aware, do not become a victim of rape while in MCU. I know you're not frightened by such warnings; I wasn't until I lived it, and I am simply saying it happens more often than it should.

As always, all things come to end. At some point and for reasons unknown, the fun I had in MCU also came to an end; it was time for me to move on. Once again, I was destined to experience another kind of misery within another abyss, just not as hot and miserable. Welcome to my experience in dorm living inside the Ada county jail.

Dorms are open living environments. There are no cages (cells) for the weak to be raped or beaten in (thank God for that). Dorms units are even louder than MCU; I would have never believed this fact until experiencing it for myself. Dorms are very dirty with out-of-control animals running wild and creating chaos within the units. Respect, what's that? Staff cares little from what I have seen. Dorm living is wall-to-wall people with pungent smells constantly in your face. Rapes are few with most homosexual acts being enacted for a price, and from what I hear, it's cheap. I will say this—it is a little better than MCU. At times even the air is a little fresher, and it doesn't smell like sweaty armpits or backed-up toilets as much as MCU. There are microwaves and flat-screen televisions. Unfortunately, the idiots who like to control the televisions also like to watch cop shows. The last thing I want to see is cops arresting others on TV while I am in jail myself—strange, right? And there are the cooking shows; I do enjoy them, but it is true torture when you are constantly starving. Ada County's dorm units also have ice machines with cold filtered water dispensers. Having access to filtered, clean water is a miracle by God while in the misery of a county jail. So I was very grateful; it was a life saver. Dorms also have a better selection of books to choose from, as I do enjoy reading. I was again very grateful to have this privilege. And remember that light above my bunk—well, it was not on as much either (I wonder why).

Dorm bathroom amenities were not much better than MCU. Instead of doing your business in front of three others, the audience was closer to ninety. The disrespectful and uncouth animals were constantly urinating on the floor and toilet seats. And when you flushed the toilet, a foul-smelling liquid came up from the floor drain, spreading a noxious odor so overpowering that it would gag even the strongest of stomachs (it somehow smelled worse than what was just flushed).

There were a few upsides in living in the dorms. One was the use of a private shower without having female staff or anyone else constantly watching you. The shower stalls were the only place to have a little privacy, to shower or cry, and of course to take care of personal business. However, one should beware, do not enter a shower stall without knocking first. Why? Because it may be occupied. This is where masturbation and hot gay action took place. Trust me, I know. I found out the hard way when I walked in on two men entangled in such romance. So if occupied, just give it a moment. Let them finish and ignore it. Everyone else does, including jail staff, who I might add, have been known to join in on such exploits.

For whatever reason, an opportunity to become an inmate worker while at Ada county jail came my way, and I eagerly accepted the offer. I excitedly moved to the inmate worker dorm that I heard was a much better place to live. It was there that I decided to write my story on paper. At that time in my life, I was broken and lost; I felt worthless as a human being and had no faith in anything, especially the justice system here in Idaho.

Time hidden away behind bars, out of the public's sight, had changed me; I was no longer optimistic and I hated everyone. I was shutting down to life, I cared for nothing other than my obsession a life-ending bullet constantly wandering the far reaches of my mind; nothing else mattered. I knew I needed help; my thinking had become erratic beyond the point of unhealthy, but the sad truth is, there was no help available, not in Ada county jail. I simply woke from a bad dream one day, knowing I had to write, that my story must be told. I knew I was no writer, but that didn't matter. I knew unquestionably that something had to be done and that I must try to bring *change* for a better America, a better Idaho. So here I am trying to do something for anyone that will listen to my story (please God, help us all). I may be a simple nobody, but it is my will to help everybody. I know my story can make a difference to others, and if it takes my life to do it, so be it. All lives matter, and when help is needed, it is my duty as a human being to help others no matter what. I will no longer make excuses for not helping; I will do my part. I will no longer be part of the problem; I will become part of the solution and no longer stand as an ostrich with my head buried in the sand. How about you, my friend? What will you be? What will you do?

I took the job in the jail kitchen working ten- to eleven-hour shifts, seven days a week, approximately 300 hours per month (give or take an hour or two). I was given one day off every thirty days of work. Now that is a lot of time spent with Satan in Hell's Kitchen, and yes, it was hell. I had three different jobs, starting in the dish pit, moving to the sandwich crew, then on to a grill cook, cooking for jail staff.

My first day in Hell's Kitchen, while hurrying across the greasy floor, I slipped. I fell, hitting my head, blacking out a few seconds, and seeing stars as I came back around. Because of treatment by medical staff once before when I had slipped and fallen (while exiting a shower a year earlier while in dorm 5), I keep my mouth shut and asked everyone who witnessed the fall to do the same. Why? Because when I had fallen in dorm 5, I went to medical and was held there for observation (a concussion precaution), an inconvenience but an understandable one. However, when I returned to dorm 5 twenty-four hours later, all my property had been stolen, gone. I wasn't going to go through that again! So because of that, I've learned to keep my mouth shut even if I was hurt (and yes, I was hurt and my head was bleeding).

I worked about a week in the dish pit; it wasn't bad. It was better than the other jobs I had while working Hell's Kitchen. I was pretty much left alone, dealing with less of the kitchen staff's hogwash and nonsense. But there was one thing that really got my attention while working the dish pit: the amount of money in food being thrown away, hundreds of pounds of food wasted, tossed in the garbage, every day, all week long. People were starving, not only in the county jail but all around the surrounding community. I knew all too well. I was one of many hundreds in that jail starving, and here I was throwing food out. It was beyond belief; I know the rescue mission or food pantries would have gladly picked up what was thrown out. If nothing else, the food could have been sold as animal feed.

Throwing out all that food was wrong, and knowing that people down the hall were starving played havoc on my mind and spirit. This was not right. How could it be when the homeless and people in the jail itself were starving? Then again, who cares about the homeless or drug-addicted, the convicted criminals, convicts, or inmates?

The money that pays for this food comes from taxpayers like you. The jail staff are but servants to the taxpayers, and that food no more belongs to them than your boss's car belongs to you. Obviously, Ada County's kitchen staff does not care. They allow this resource to be squandered, wasted, and thrown away each and every day of the year (these are your tax dollars being thrown away). Unbeknownst to me, besides washing pots and pans without any soap, my job while working in the dish pit was to throw out food, lots of food. One morning, while talking to a member of the kitchen staff, I asked about soap. I was told soap was none of my business, and then I was threatened, if I didn't get back work immediately I would be rolled up for disrespecting staff. (Fired and moved back to MCU). I heard the threat loud and clear, and it was in that moment I realized I was nothing but a cog in the wheel of a gigantic carceration state. What I thought, felt, or knew was irrelevant. I learned once again to keep my mouth shut while working in Hell's Kitchen.

So yes, I kept my mouth shut no matter what, even when the milk deliveries came in each week with expired dates on the cartons. I would stock the walk-in refrigerator with expired milk cartons one day, only to be told to throw it away the next, and in the trash it went. Week after week, I did what I was told, throwing away good hard-earned tax dollars. This madness of waste had been going on long before I came along, and it will continue. My hope is that this book exposes this waste, but I need your help to stop it. Another thing I found strange was that the cold cereal not only came from Mexico but that the cereal was also always expired. Then again, who buys expired cold cereal by the cases from Mexico? One would think tax-payers' dollars would be spent here in America, supporting American and local jobs. Idaho's Ada County jail doesn't even buy local potatoes. They don't even buy spuds from Idaho, but instead, they buy out-of-state potatoes. What could possibly be more disrespectful to the Idaho taxpayer who is shelling out the very money that supports the Ada county jail than that?

I have seen the ugly truth: I know how the kitchen staff handles detainees' food. Sanitary has no place in this county-run kitchen. Handwashing is virtually nonexistent inside. Cleanliness and health are of little concern. Rodents have run of the entire kitchen area, so be careful, you may trip over one (not to mention the two-legged rats in red shirts that are constantly looking for their handout of cheese). It truly is Hell's Kitchen.

Come all, see for yourself. It may appear clean and sanitized upon first sight, with gloves and hairnets worn, but under further inspection, you will see gloves and hair nets tossed aside with scurrying mice, insects, and spreading mold creeping in every darkened corner. Inmates' food trays are frequently left uncovered for hours, and leftovers are rarely covered once placed in walk-in refrigerators and freezers. Frozen items left out to be thawed are often forgotten or unused, only to be refrozen again, over and over, until one day used in the detainees' meals. Food labels have main ingredients that I have never even heard of and are often unreadable or impossible to pronounce, containing items such as *hydrogenated corn oil* and *texture vegetable protein* (TVP) and are often labeled *Not for Human Consumption* (unless *cooked* is usually added in small lettering). I still have problems believing this, even after holding the labels myself. Inmates are actually being fed hog slop for pigs and other animals. Turkey franks (hotdogs) that are being served in the jail are not turkey, nor do they have the equivalent amount of meat for a child. The last time I checked, Ada county jail was an adult facility and not meant to hold or feed children.

The food being served in the Ada county jail has nowhere close to the daily required nutritional value for an adult. All meals are based on calories, and the majority of all calories come from sugar, hydrogenated oil, and lard, meaning cookies and cakes. This is not healthy for anyone. I for one couldn't eat the majority of what was being served in this jail. I was in a constant battle with diarrhea and/or constipation. No matter what I did, I couldn't win; it was a never-ending battle. This played havoc on my body, and in time, I lost an average of forty-four pounds. The last time held there, I came out weighing 132 pounds (even after working in the kitchen). This was in no way a healthy weight for me; I was skin and bones. I felt like crap and looked tired, beaten, and worn (it is what it is, when in jail).

The women who manage and operate Hell's Kitchen (during my time there) are truly controlling demons sent by Satan himself. They seldom wear hair and beard nets and are oblivious to leaving hair in detainees' food (some of these woman honestly need beard nets). They are constantly barking orders, yelling and screaming, creating unwarranted havoc and stress on inmate workers. Inmate workers are continually threatened with roll-ups (threats of being fired and moved back to MCU) for trying to do a job that no one trained them to do.

I also know of one Ada county kitchen staff employee who engaged in oral sex with inmates, right in the staff's office (you know how you are, the blond one). Sexual innuendos were commonplace for both sides, the braver inmates wanting to find their way to the staff office and the staff wanting to get them there. One staff member began calling me Pretty Boy. To her I would like to say thanks for making me feel uncomfortable and weird while I was trying to do my job. Sexual harassment and sexism is not appropriate in any form, anywhere.

Do not think this type of activity does not go on or happen. A staff member was recently fired and criminally charged at an Idaho prison for having sex with an inmate (2014, in the 24 House bathroom). In another well-known case, a female Idaho juvenile correctional officer was fired and jailed, and the state of Idaho sued her after she molested several underage boys at the juvenile detention center in Nampa, Idaho. And let's not forget the two inmates that escaped from a New York prison after compromising a female guard there. In a more recent case (March of 2016), a nurse was escorted off Idaho prison grounds after being compromised by a known predator, an inmate convicted of killing and burning his girlfriend's body.

Most detainees would wear this type of sexual conduct as a badge of honor, and I am sure some reading this may believe this type of activity is no big deal. However, compromised staff endangers both staff and inmates. This type of activity frequently creates jealousy between inmates suspecting others are receiving special privileges from staff, and such suspicions often end in violence. Staff may be blackmailed or extorted (remember the New York escapees) or be talked into bringing drugs or other contraband into the facility while inmates may be denied probation, parole, or face additional charges.

One deputy sheriff at the Twin Falls county jail was suspended after bailing out young women for sexual favors. This deputy sheriff was actually turing young troubled women into prostitutes. This deputy sheriff has not only been reinstated and is currently back to work at the county jail, he has since then been promoted.

In addition to throwing taxpayers' dollars out (throwing food out) while working in Hell's kitchen, I also delivered meals throughout the jail. As I was doing my job, I witnessed many inhumane and cold-hearted things. For instance, every time I went to the medical unit (Hospitable Security Unit, or HSU), I saw detainees locked in cages, screaming and crying for help, covered in their own feces and/or blood (head to toe). And yes, this made me throw up. What stood out to me was how disrespectful the sheriff deputies were to these suffering human beings. At times, I would come onto the unit to find staff at their desk reading a magazine or surfing the Internet without a care of what was going on around them. The insanity of it all was very disturbing—delusional inmates screaming and crying, some painfully, fearfully, or violently lashing out, yelling out in distress as guards callously read magazines while eating their lunches. The horror of it all tormented me, twisted my thoughts, and sickened my mind. To this day, I can still hear the screams echoing in my dreams.

One time, when delivering meals to the Twilight Zone (HSU), there was a woman. She was young— early twenties I would say. She had no legs and was sitting in a wheelchair, but what I found most disturbing was the way she was restrained. Though one of her arms was shorter than the other (much shorter), she was handcuffed. The restraints forced her to hold her body in an awkward position, giving the scene a very odd and unusual appearance to me. When I witnessed this, it made me sick to my stomach, even forcing tears to my eyes. It didn't make any sense to me. Why would a young girl with obvious disabilities (no legs, in a wheelchair, and malformed arms) be locked in a cage and handcuffed in such a way? The only logical reason I could think of for treating her in such disrespectful and inhumane way was that the county deputy sheriffs must have been very afraid of this young girl with no legs. To be honest, this was the saddest thing I have ever seen.

Becoming an inmate worker at the Ada county jail does have its benefits, somewhat. One can earn up to ten dollars every two weeks (living large). You do work your hind end off for it, but this is not considered a payment for your work; it is merely an incentive to work. If you were paid to work, then state and federal work laws would apply—minimum wage, workman's compensation, and unemployment benefits, among other things. So beware, if you are ever in a position to accept this offer to work, be very careful not to get hurt or fired. Do not get sucked into inmates' games (or the kitchen staff's office for sex); don't mess up or else. If by chance, for whatever reasons, you get fired, rolled up, or even quit your job, it can and more than likely will be used against you at your sentencing by the prosecuting attorney. I know because I have seen it too many times while I was waiting my turn in court.

There is another side to the Ada county jail kitchen. This other side feeds all the jail staff who work there. The majority of all the money being spent on food that comes into the jail is for staff dining. I will be honest. Staff are not always eating food that is compromised with inmates' spittle and fecal matter—nope, not always, just most of the time (though I myself never compromised staff food). I had a co-worker—every morning he would go to the bathroom, jack off into a cup, and use his sperm (cum) as a butter for jail staff pancakes and French toast (yum, yum). When I was a child, I learned early on to never piss on or piss off the *cook*. I'm just saying, it's good advice to live by!

Staff dining is first class, with fresh fruit and vegetables, beef steak, boneless skinless chicken, pork, eggs, bacon, sausages, real cheese, and much more. I guarantee Ada county jail staff is eating better than a majority of Idaho's citizens. Why not? It's free to them. But guess who pays the bill? If you guessed you, the Idaho taxpayer, you would be right. By the way, most of this food is also wasted, thrown away at the end of the day.

Ada county jail staff refer to the detainees/inmates as animals, and when it comes to feeding of the animals, all hot meals are delivered in filthy, unsanitary hot carts. Meals are left in hot carts for hours before they are delivered to their destination. By the time the animals receive their meals, they are ruined, dried out. The majority of it is thrown away because of this, causing a hunger that creates stress, which in return promotes the havoc that incites so much of Ada county jails' violence. It's a vicious cycle to live in; I know, because I have seen what it does. Obviously jail staff is aware of this but does nothing to help prevent it. This madness puts the weak in danger and lives at risk (people are often beaten for their meals). Trust me, if someone asks you if you want your cornbread, it might be best to just let them have it.

Beside the deplorable living conditions at the Ada county jail, Fourth Amendment rights are nonexistent. While being detained inside the jail, you are subject to shakedowns at any given time (searches of person, property, and living areas). These searches include your property box, your bunk, your living area, and of course, your anal cavity. As I have made aware earlier in this chapter, I have been given the pleasure of the finger search by the same sheriff's deputy many times. Although I have already made this clear, I will say again that this type of search is not fun. It is a humiliating violation of one's dignity.

There is no respect shown or given by jail staff during these searches. Overly priced hygiene and commissary food items are spilled and poured out, therefore wasting them (trust me, jail house commissary is the ultimate price gouging). Inmates are left feeling violated, angered to the point of infuriated when jail staff leaves their overly priced food items scattered across the floor. Jail staff's indignant behavior during and after these searches creates tension between the staff and inmate population. Unfortunately it is what it is and it will never change—unless, just maybe, someone gets killed.

Being a detainee in the Ada county jail, one is denied the small human pleasures taken for granted when at home, like the luxury of being able to shave with a clean razor. Ada County jail is famously known for handing out used razors to its inmates, spreading blood-borne pathogens such as Hepatitis C and AIDS. Not willing to take a chance with my life, I was forced to live without shaving, and for me, this was not an easy thing. It played havoc on my mind and spirit. And remember when I was suffering with diarrhea, my rectum became so raw it bled from the use of the eighty-grit sandpaper pretending to be toilet paper. I had heard others refer to Ada County's toilet paper as John Wayne paper, saying it doesn't take crap off anyone, but I might argue that because it seemed to remove my skin!

There were many situations in which I, as well as others, became victims of someone else's actions while in the Ada county jail. Yes, we all suffered (as a group) the punishment given by jail staff. This practice is known as group punishment, and it is illegal. If one person is suspected of something or does something to annoy or anger jail staff, all pay the price, the consequences. Though illegal, this is common practice in both jails and prisons. Sheriffs, wardens, and staff will deny this type of punishment takes place, but ask anyone that has spent any time behind bars; they will tell you just as I have.

All mail coming into a jail or prison facility is opened, searched for contraband, and scanned (or read) for key words indicating escape attempts, riots, and other security issues. But the Ada county jail makes a common practice out of opening outgoing mail as well (most jails do not unless it is part of an ongoing investigation, usually looking into gang activity). Though I have never had any part in any kind of gang activity and there was no ongoing investigation in my case (that I knew of), I stopped sending mail out because my letters were not reaching their destinations, and if they did, though my home was less than two miles from the jail, it could take up to several weeks. Let this be a warning for all, be very careful in what is being said in the writing of words on paper in the Ada county jail. Words are twisted and they can and will be used against you in a court of law (trust me, I know, I've witnessed it first-hand). It is a dirty trick played by the district attorney's office to ensure guilty pleas and plea deals offered by prosecutors, and it works very well for them.

Following rules has always been easy for me. Most rules are common sense (one would hope anyway), and I have never had a problem with that, especially in a structured environment such as a jail or prison. In all my time behind walls, within a jail or prison, not once have I ever been addressed or disciplined for any negative or disrespectful behavior toward staff or anyone else. However, within my first two hours of arrival at the Ada county jail, I was threatened with disciplinary action.

When first arriving at the Ada county jail, I was handed some paperwork that I was asked to sign. As I began to go over this paperwork, I noticed it said that I had received and read the Ada county handbook of policy and procedures (Ada County's rulebook). I had not seen one of these publications and thought such a handbook could be helpful to me, and I asked to see one. The booking officer said most new arrivals cared little for the rulebook and that everyone usually signed this form without seeing one. Though I was in no way disrespectful when I stated that I still wanted to see their policy and procedure handout, the officer moaned his disapproval, shuffled some paperwork around, and then told me to sign the form or face disciplinary action.

Within my first hours of arriving in this jail, to this day I have never seen or read one, I was always forced to sign papers saying I had received and read the Ada county jail's policy and procedures handbook (rulebook). This was not true, and it is a type of blackmail. It is fraud by deception, and it is a form of corruption.

Ada county jail has a resource center, a law library (though they may claim they do, many counties in Idaho, such as Twin Falls, do not have any such resource center or library). I was not getting the help I believed I was entitled to or any useful information from my public defender and decided I would try to help myself by learning what I could in the law library. What I learned was the State of Idaho had intentionally made case law/precedent unavailable to inmates who wished to proceed *Pro se* (defend themselves). The lack of this information makes it impossible for any inmate to argue his/her case with any reasonable standard of adequacy. The Ada county law library was of no help to me or anyone else—unless you are looking for law history from the years 1891–1975.

America spent two billion tax dollars fighting for women's rights in the Middle East (Iraq and Afghanistan). I am not saying that human or women's rights are not important or worth investing in, but the American taxpayer arrested and charged of a crime in the United States consults with their public defender on an average of three minutes and has no access to current information in the very land they live in because there is no money for such luxuries. This makes no sense to me whatsoever.

Because there are no funds for proper counsel or resource centers, and due to the need of free inmate labor, and the greed of politicians handing out local and state contracts for kickbacks in the way of campaign contributions, a majority of the people leaving the Ada county jail and other jail facilities across the United States are heading to prison. Ada county jail, as well as other county facilities I am told, seems to take pleasure in using this opportunity to punish you one last time. For whatever their reasons, the Ada county jail destroys what property you have stored with them. This means whatever you came in with—clothing, shoes and everything else you had when arrested—is destroyed, including your wallet, identification card, driver's license, social security card, and everything else, leaving you with nothing when released from prison.

As I have mentioned before, I came into the Ada county jail hurt, suffering from a pinched nerve in my neck and shoulder area. This injury was causing numbness in my left arm all the way down to my fingertips. I was under a doctor's care at the time of my arrest and had my medical records sent to the jail's medical provider confirming my injury. Unfortunately, it did no good. Trying to get any medical treatment was useless. Other than being seen by some kind of nurse practitioner who wanted to give me pain pills, I was refused and ignored.

The answer to all medical issues in the Ada county jail is a pill. I refused to take a narcotic; therefore, I went without any real medical treatment for my injury. Medical treatment is not provided unless you are bleeding or dying, then just maybe, you might see one of their non-doctors (maybe). The medical provider in the Ada county jail received the contract because they gave the lowest bid (fee enterprise right). We are all aware that the lowest bid may mean fewer services, but in this case, it means as little as possible.

In 1976, US Supreme Court ruled that failure to provide appropriate medical care to prisoners amounted to a violation of the US constitution prohibition on cruel and unusual punishment. The sad truth is, many incarceration people simply don't receive medical treatment.

In many circumstances, medical problems addressed early can be most effectively treated. When inmates are forced to go months (sometimes longer) without treatment, injuries and existing problems often become complicated and require additional treatment. They also end in law suits costing the state hundreds of thousands, sometimes even millions. Scott, an Iraqi war hero (literally, he was awarded for his bravery and valor both before and during his capture in Iraq) won a twenty-two-million-dollar lawsuit after being refused treatment for cancer in both the Ada county jail and an Idaho prison. Lowest bid or not, to refuse anyone medical treatment, without question, is wrong.

Seldom does anything good ever happen while being held in the Ada county jail. For me, I was blessed week after week for months at the end of my last visit, with free phone time. It would mystically appear on my account, and it was always the same amount. I would like to say "thank you" to the incompetent person who did the banking and tell them that they were doing a great job.

Obviously going to jail can be a traumatic experience for anyone. I had a complete mental, physical, emotional, and social meltdown every time I came back into this jail. Every time back it started right where I left off, and I was far from being OK. I pray to God every day for the help to overcome the torment I was subjected to by the hands of a carceration state. Nevertheless, Ada county jail is but a tip of the iceberg, the majority of the problems and dangers lie under the surface safely hidden from public scrutiny, waiting to overturn and crush this great country and its citizens . . .

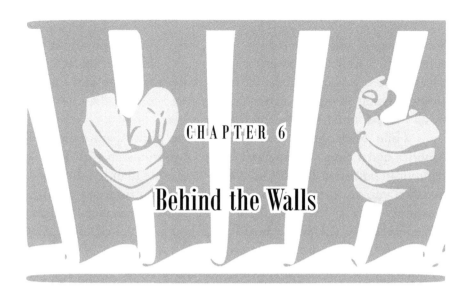

CHAPTER 6

Behind the Walls

M any communities across America rely heavily on the prison system for employment. Idaho communities are no different, and in fact, when considering probation and parole (P&P), the parole board, and all contractors that significantly rely on lucrative awarded Idaho contracts. The Idaho prison system is among the greatest employers of Idaho's citizens.

Idaho's prisons are always full, maxed-out beyond capacity. After you have been sentenced to prison by a Judge you may wait months or years in a county jail before being transferred to an Idaho prison facility. In Idaho, at any given time, there are hundreds of poor souls, newly convicted inmates waiting in county jails, waiting for a bus ride to prison. Depending on your location, it could take either days or less than an hour to reach the infamous prison row of Idaho.

Prison row consists of eight separate facilities (though some are only separated by fencing), each a different security level prison facility. Each one is separate with its own identity and operation. Driving south from Boise, the first building one notices on prison row is the Idaho State Correctional Center (ISCC). ISCC holds about 2,500 inmates and was once known as the Idaho Correctional Corporations (ICC), one of the sixty-five private prisons throughout the United

States owned and operated by the Correction Corporations of America (CCA). CCA also owns and operates three private facilities overseas. ICC prison in Idaho is famously known as one of the most violent prisons in our country. ICC is referred to as gladiator school by all Idaho's inmates including IDOC.

While operating in Idaho, the Corrections Corporation of America had a close working and financial relationship with Idaho's republican governor, Butch Otter, donating more than ten thousand dollars a year to Otter's campaign fund. It is also rumored, though I cannot verify at this time, that many Idaho lawmakers, judges, and members of the parole board itself had an invested interest in Correction Corporation of America, a direct conflict of interest, enticing all to pass laws or deny parole to protect their interest.

Inmate beatings and lawsuits were a constant norm for the Idaho Correctional Corporations. ICC was originally built to house a medium-security population. However, toward the end of their operation, ICC housed minimum-, medium-, and maximum-security inmates. Often, the most troubling and hard to deal with inmates were housed at ICC, creating security risk to both inmates and undermanned as well as undertrained staff. Idaho was fully aware of these problems but ignored this fact. Two of ICC's violent outbursts were caught on videotape, both making national news. In one, an inmate was repeatedly beaten and stomped by another inmate. This attack went on without officers' response for so long that the attacker actually stopped and sat down, resting, getting something to drink before continuing the attack. The beaten inmate was in a program where he was forced to write tickets on other inmates (considered by some to be tattling or snitching), and was supposedly beaten in retaliation for doing so. He was left with severe brain damage and later died of complications due to the violent beating. Another violent attack caught on tape was a gang war exploding in the heart of the thunder-dome itself, ICC's JKL unit.

Though there were many gang-related incidents at ICC, the gang war caught on tape made national news. One new arrival was attempting to create a new gang, angering existing gangs, erupting into a war. Though this was big news across Idaho, little was actually done by prison officials. And if not for the videotape, sadly, it is my sincere belief even less would have been done.

Those were just two incidents caught on tape; there were many others jeopardizing inmate's health and security and costing millions in lawsuits. One such case involved a man named Riggs. Mr. Riggs was placed in ICC's thunder-dome (the JKL unit), where he was told by gang members that he had to move off the unit. Riggs went to staff and informed them that he had to move; staff immediately asked why. Fearing retaliation, Riggs informed officers that he could not tell them why. (There is no place safe from others at ICC, and anyone suspected of snitching or telling on others is definitely targeted.) Officers refused Riggs's request because he would not snitch, and he was sent back to his cell where he was later beaten unconscious, leaving him permanently suffering blurred vision and severe headaches. Riggs filed a lawsuit for one hundred and eighty million dollars ($180,000,000), one year's profit for Correction Corporation of America. The lawsuit was later settled for an undisclosed amount.

In 2013, CCA handed back prison operations to the State of Idaho after a scandal that cost the Idaho's taxpayers millions. A one-million-dollar settlement was paid to Idaho by CCA (much less than what was stolen from Idaho's taxpayer by CCA). And the US attorney for the state of Idaho did nothing about this crime against Idaho; no charges were ever filed against CCA. The question is, why not? It is the belief of many that Idaho law makers did not run CCA out of Idaho as they, Butch Otter and others claim, but that CCA was not profitable in the state and paid their way out in a way that was comfortable for all. Unfortunately for Idaho tax payers, once IDOC/Idaho gained control of the CCA facility, the prison budget was raised from $180,000,000 to a record $212,000,000 a year for the takeover, matching the total school budget for the entire state of Idaho. You have to ask yourself, what kind of nation have we become when education takes a back seat to incarceration?

To the northwest of ISCC sits the old slaughterhouse, a facility that was once used to process beef for the prison, due to jail staff incompetence and theft of inmates food (beef), beef production has been stopped and the building renovated into living quarters for low-custody-level inmates working jobs in the community, a community work center (CWC) or community re-entry center (CRC). Though the state will deny this fact, community work release inmates generate huge amounts of income for the state of Idaho. (This is mass incarceration for profit.) Inmates are charged thirty percent of their gross income (before state and federal taxes), plus four dollars for each ride, each way to and from work (usually eight dollars a day), and an additional eight dollars a month for use of washers and dryers. In most cases, this adds up to about 50 percent of the inmates' pay. The prison staff is kept to a minimum and low custody level inmate's work as janitors, maintenance workers, kitchen help, and even drivers to take inmates to and from work; all are paid eighty dollars a month. When one considers these work centers are taking half the income, it does not take a mathematician to see there is a huge profit margin in such facilities. There are two other such facilities in Idaho for men and another for women, with plans to reopen another men's facility in Twin Falls after an existing one there closed during the housing market crash and following recession. There are approximately one hundred inmates held in each one of Idaho's work release centers.

Continuing south from ISCC, you will find Idaho's last remaining private-owned prison, a minimum security facility owned and operated by Management and Training Corporation (MTC), known as the CAPP program. MTC has an ongoing financial relationship with Idaho politicians. Governor Butch Otter (Republican) (approximately the same amount he received from CCA), House Judiciary Rules Administration Committee Representative, Rich Wills (Republican—Glenn's Ferry) receives two hundred and fifty dollars a year, and fellow committee member Representative Luke Malek (Republican—Coeur d'Alene) also receives two hundred and fifty dollars a year. The CAPP program was intended as an alternative to prison for parole violators and low-level, first-time offenders. As with everything else to do with the prison system, it has become distorted, and though it is still used for these purposes, it is often used for things never intended or designed for.

Directly across from ISCC (to the east) stands a large entrance gate with a department of corrections sign above it, just inside of which you will find one of the two women facilities found on prison row. This first building serves as a community custody facility, a work center in which women may go to work in the community, again generating huge amounts of money for the state of Idaho and saving a small amount for the inmate workers. It also serves as a women's violator center, an alternative to prison for women found guilty of violating probation or parole.

Just up from the women's work center looms one of Idaho's two maximum security facilities for men, the Idaho Maximum Security Institution (IMSI) and the other maximum facility is located in Orofino, Idaho. IMSI was intended to separate Idaho's most dangerous criminals from the lower-level inmates, but this too has become muddled. IMSI has become a segregation facility for inmates who receive multiple or serious Disciplinary Order Reports (DORs), more than it is to separate the higher-level offenders, thus allowing murderers and rapist to roam freely among inmates convicted of low-level drug offences and DUIs. The Idaho Maximum Security Institution also houses inmates sentenced to death, and the execution chamber is located just behind IMSI.

Continuing east, the next compound seen is the Southern Idaho Correctional Institution (SICI or the Farm), a minimum custody facility for men. Though still a working compound, the farm used to be used as just that, a farm. SICI inmates used to raise cattle and grow much of the prison's food supply, but corruption and lucrative government contracts handed out for kickbacks in the way of campaign contributions put a stop to that. However, SICI is still a working compound in which men can work state jobs, such as fire crews and other forest service jobs. Inmates also work with local highway departments and the nearby air force base (Gowen Field) and are also contracted out to a local orchard. As of recently (2018) Idaho inmates are now being contracted out into the community to a local beef packing plant. Just down the road from prison row. IDOC is profiting hand over fist from this lucrative contract, and paying no taxes. All these jobs pay very little to the inmate working them, starting at thirty cents an hour, up to one dollar and twenty-five cents for the higher-paying fire crew jobs. There is also no workman's compensation or unemployment benefits paid, which creates or saves huge amounts of money for the state of Idaho. These jobs are often vital to a state's economy, so important that California voters overwhelming passed laws to release low-level offenders held in California State Prisons, but the prison officials and state lawmakers refused, stating that California could not afford to release inmates working state jobs. Truth is, the majority of all states are in the same position; they can't afford to give up their free labor force or what many would call as slave labor. Nevertheless, I have heard it said that for every man working one of these jobs, there are two families starving: the family of the inmate working it and the family of the man that should be working it. There are roughly four hundred inmates held at the farm working these jobs.

Adjoined to SICI compound, you will find the second of the two women's facilities, a minimum-security facility for the women's Rider Program, a program offering an alternative to long-term prison sentences. Rather than being sentenced to lengthy stays in prison, the Rider Program offers men and women, usually first-time offenders and probation violators, a chance to complete a program and be released on probation. However, statistics show more than eighty percent of riders return to prison within a year. The success rates of these programs (Thinking for a Change [TFAC], Cognitive Behavioral Interventions—Substance Abuse [CBI-SA], and Aggression Replacement Training [ART]) are intentionally being manipulated by the prison system. They are running people through like sheep. This is truly fraud by deception and a waste of good, hard-earned tax dollars. Truth is the Rider treatment program is a complete and utter failure, and yet IDOC continues to waste tax dollars on a failed treatment program—I wonder why?

The next stop on prison row is Idaho State Correctional Institution (ISCI), also known as the Yard. The yard holds about 1,750 inmates and is the beginning of everyone's prison career in Idaho. Idaho's prisoner intake, or Reception and Diagnostic Unit (RDU), is located in one of the ten housing units spread across the yard. When you step off the prison bus, you enter the yard through seven-house (old death row). There, restraints are removed and another strip search is conducted before you are handed a white or yellow jumpsuit. The color of jumpsuit identifies you as a timer or a program rider. Riders stay in seven-house while timers are moved to B dorm in fifteen-house for classification.

This initial classification determines where you may be housed (your new home). Your custody level is based on a points system. My points put me in a minimum/community custody (my points were on the low side). While in RDU, you go through orientation and many types of screenings. Finger printing and photographs are taken of your entire body (tattoos), and DNA tests are done. You also receive your prison identification card with your prison number printed across it (this number is yours for life). There is also medical, dental, and mental health (which is new in recent years) evaluations and screenings. Drug and alcohol assessments, education screening, and a pathway/program plans are assigned. Warden and security briefings are conducted, along with gender identification screenings. You are also briefed on maintaining your dignity, part of the Prison Rape and Elimination Act (PREA). All inmates should have the opportunity to serve their sentence with dignity (sadly many inmates do not). All these screening and evaluations take about a week to complete. Unfortunately, prison beds are occupied; you may wait weeks or months in RDU waiting for a bed to open and move forward to another facility or housing unit.

During my medical screening, while I was being given a physical, the doctor cupped my scrotum in his cold hand and told me to cough. After the examination, the doctor tells me he is referring me to a mental health clinician, I said nothing at the time. A day later, I was called out of my cage to a mental health clinician's office. I knocked on the door and heard a woman's voice asking me to come on in and take a seat. I did what I was asked without saying a word. She was sitting at a desk reading a file (I was assuming it was mine). A few moments later, she put the file down and looked up at me. "The doctor had some concerns. He said you would not look at him during your medical exam."

Surprised by this, I gave the woman a confused look, thinking, *How embarrassing this is.* Though uncomfortable talking to a woman, I said, "The man had my genitals in his hand and I wasn't gonna watch him play with my balls during the exam. It didn't feel right. It felt very weird to me."

Toward the end of our conversation, she asked if I needed anything to help me sleep at night, referring to some kind of medication. "Nope, I'm good," I quickly replied, surprising her. Most inmates do not pass an opportunity for medication, and the prison is quick to hand it out. Idaho medicates their inmates population much higher than the national average. It is a quick fix for medical staff, clinicians, and officers overseeing inmate population but a terrible practice for the inmates themselves.

My next step in the intake process was with a nurse commonly known to Idaho inmates as the Vampire. Most were not particularly fond of the vampire, a woman with a thick Russian or Bosnian accent who seemed to enjoy sucking the blood of others for a living. During my blood draw, she stabbed me three times in one arm and four times in the other. I was bruised for weeks from her careless stabbings. Many inmates (IV drug users) joked about drawing their own blood to avoid the painful bruising of the vampire.

After all the poking, stabbing, prodding, and testing is complete, the waiting begins. RDU inmates spend most of the day in their cells. Boredom creeps in as thoughts churn. Books are few, phone calls are often hard or impossible to make, and thoughts of family, loved ones, and regret frequently surface, causing discontent in many of the new arrivals.

Prison is many things to different kinds of people. Depending on who you talk to, it can be considered Disneyland, Pris-ney-land, Daddy Day Care, or Adult Day Care. *Idiotville, Stupid Land,* and *Clown College* are among the words often used to describe Idaho's prison system. Some consider it a state mental hospital, funny farm, or an insane asylum. Others think of it as one big, gay orgy party; others a senior citizens' center or old folks' home (due to Idaho's lengthy sentences, Idaho prisons house a large number of older inmates).

Inmates from other states will compare Idaho's prison system to their past home states, saying things like "Idaho does not have a real prison" or things like "If this were a real prison." The truth is that Idaho's prison system may be different than many states, especially ones with a more diverse inmate population. A majority of Idaho's population is Caucasian (white); therefore, Idaho does not have the racial divide of most prisons in the United States. However, Idaho prisons do have a disproportionately large Hispanic and African-American population compared to the state's general population. Idaho also sentences inmates convicted of minor crimes to lengthy prison terms, such as simple possession, something that most states would consider a misdemeanor or wouldn't bother with at all, which also creates a more passive inmate population. However, whatever word is used to describe Idaho's prison system, or whatever your views are on its inmate population, I assure you that Idaho prisons are indeed prisons.

For some it has become a home away from home; for others, it's a way of life (institutionalized). But to me, living in a prison is the same as living in a petri-dish, infested with every sexually transmitted disease known to mankind. Prison is a criminal college, a university for all (especially the young) to learn and become a professional criminal for life at taxpayers' expense. I assure you that Idaho prisons are no joke. They are hellholes, a waiting room for the damned.

When first sentenced to prison, I had no idea what the real rules were, the unspoken inmate rules. Sure, there is a prison handbook. A handout is provided to help smooth the period of adjustment and transition into prison life, but there is no unspoken rule handbook. There is no how-to booklet on prison etiquette, nothing on the knowledge or behavior needed to live behind the walls. Everything I have learned was by trial and error. Believe me, it was rough going for many months as I learned everything the hard way.

The first time in RDU, I spent six weeks in a cage with a non-English-speaking gentleman. The only thing I understood was that this was also his first time in prison (we both had that in common). Once my classification was done, I was sent to ICC, a private prison. The Idaho Correctional Center, or ICC, was still owned and operated by Corrections Corporation of America (CCA) at that time. During my stay at ICC, I witnessed the violence firsthand. I have seen how understaffing played into the violence within the walls and how ICC staff allowed and used prison gangs to create fear and turmoil, to control and keep the so-called order inside the prison facility. I witnessed ICC staff do nothing to stop violent acts in progress. They simply watched, allowing it to continue on like it was their entertainment value for the day.

My first housing placement at ICC was in a sex offender program unit. I am not a sex offender, nor have I ever been charged or convicted of a sex-related offense. I immediately began to address my concerns with prison staff, continuing week after week only to be ignored. During that time other inmates watched me, the new *fish* (a term used for new arrivals) came and went from a sex offender program unit. I did not know this at the time, but ICC staff had painted a giant bull's eye in the middle of my back. After learning this fact I packed up my property and placed it all by the unit door, blocking it. This got the attention of prison staff. Once again I had to explain my situation, but this time I was not giving up. Not only did I get the prison staff's attention, I got hundreds of inmates' attention as well.

Once staff understood I was not giving up, I was moved to the unit next door. This was not a sex offender program unit. Unfortunately, the damage was done; I just didn't know of it just then. Something was off, wrong. I was immediately paper checked (asked for my sentencing paperwork showing the crimes I had been convicted of). Unfortunately, I did not have any paperwork; I had sent it home not knowing I would need it again. This was not good; I was just out of a sex offender program unit with no paperwork to show my criminal history or who I was, a clear violation of prisoner etiquette.

I was not prepared for this nor did I know what to do about it. I knew by inmates' attitudes that something bad was about to happen, but other than knowing it was about to happen to me, I had no idea what it was going to be. I was left feeling overwhelmed with fear and anxiety. About a week later, I was called out by staff and told I was being moved to another housing unit across the hall. This could not have come at a better time, a definite relief to my stress and anxiety levels.

As I was packing my property, I noticed a few haters snickering and pointing in my direction. Their actions did not alarm me much at that moment; I was on my way out the door, leaving them and this hellhole behind. However, I learned another lesson the hard way: never assume, never turn your back, and never think it doesn't matter, because everything matters inside the walls.

Not paying attention to my surrounding and what was going on around me, three young men, no older than twenty-five, snuck up on me while still in my bunk area and demanded that I surrender my radio for rent. I simply said no. Immediately, one of them threw a wild punch, but I jerked and he completely missed me. I charged the closest, taking him down to the floor in the corner of the bunk area, his two buddies immediately fleeing, leaving him. I did what I had to do to defend myself, no more, no less.

Adrenaline is a powerful thing. I did well standing my ground, confronting the other two that took off after allowing the one I had taken down back up. They had nothing more to say and did nothing. I knew my side bunkie had talked them into this. Though I did not understand this at the time, this type of activity is a game often played by younger inmates. This is too often the perception of how one should act by many younger inmates, and they are easily talked into doing such things by the older inmates who enjoy watching the violence.

Though staff was unaware of what had taken place, the commotion (probably my yelling) did bring them onto the unit. I allowed my heart rate to calm a second before quietly grabbing my property and leaving the unit. Once outside the door, staff questioned about the yelling.

"Seriously," I snarled, "there are five of you standing here with your thumbs in your butts while less than five feet away I was being robbed and assaulted, and you want to know why I was yelling!"

I was immediately tackled by prison security, smashing my head down on the concrete floor as they restrained my hands with handcuffs. I was then carried off to another part of the prison, the Hole.

The hole is a solitary confinement cell, a jail within a prison. I was left alone and handcuffed for well over twelve hours before anyone came to see or talk with me about what had taken place.

By this time, I was not at all happy about how I was being treated. I did my best to explain the situation, informing the investigating officer that I did not know the names of others involved, nor did I think I would recognize them (remember, snitching inside the walls is taboo). What I did come to understand is that I should not have talked to the officers at all, that I should have kept my big mouth shut. No one would have known what had happened on the tier, and I would not have been handcuffed and stuffed in a cage with a head'ache from a concussion. It was on that day that I learned to never talk to officers or inmates, no matter what. From that day forward, I understood that talking about anything that happened to me or witnessed by me meant paying a very high price. I knew talking would mean taxation (punishment) by inmates and/or police. From that day forward, I knew nothing, period. And I have kept my mouth shut ever since, no matter what.

I sat in that cage (the hole) for thirty-one days without having a shower or clean clothes. I ate and slept on a concrete slab without a mattress. My cage had no windows, and the only way I could tell time was by meals being served. I had no way to communicate with my family, nor was I given my mail.

It was on the thirty-first day that I was pulled out of my cage and taken to an office where a prison staff member informed me of my rights during a DOR (Disciplinary Order Report) hearing. Not understanding any of this or what was going on at the time, I simply just agreed (basically pleading guilty without knowledge of it). It was then I found out I was written up for fighting, and I was given a class A DOR for this fight. Confused by all of this, I tried to explain it was I who was attacked, that not only was I defending myself (self-defense), but after the fact, it was also I who reported the situation to staff.

Of course I was found guilty; after all, I partially admitted to fighting before the hearing began. Nevertheless, the sad truth is that there was nothing I could have said or done at that time. ICC had a huge problem with violence and gang activity, and officers had already found me guilty in their minds. They are constantly lied to by inmates, and their truth was reached long before I entered the room.

At that time, I was told I would be going back to the same unit. I immediately questioned this madness, refusing to go back to the same place and risk being assaulted again. I was hauled off, back to my cage for another five days. I spent thirty-six days in that cage, scared and confused by what was going on. I felt terrible; I was in both mental and physical chaos. I reeked of body odor; my skin was dry, my hair greasy, and my mind wandered in torment. Everything I went through was because I did not know the unspoken prison rules. I learned the hard way (it is what it is). On the thirty-sixth day, I was moved to the north wing area of the prison. Because of this DOR, I lost all privileges—no commissary and no visits for ninety days, plus I was reclassified and my custody level points went up (not good). My first ninety days in prison was nothing but turmoil and total madness. I made the mistake of trusting prison staff. That's on me; never again will I ever trust anyone who works for the system.

Ironically, a few years later, I was placed in a strange situation after being brought back to ICC's. I came face to face with the ring leader who had sent the three wannabe gang members (the three kids that had attacked me) to strong-arm me and steal my radio. Long story short, this man did not recognize me, but I knew exactly who he was (a very dangerous situation for someone doing time). Fortunately for both of us, staff intervened, coming between us before things got out of hand. I explained my actions, and surprisingly, staff understood. I found out later, though he had probably gotten the disease from sharing dirty insulin needles stolen from medical, that man had been raping many of the young, new arrivals and had contracted AIDS. I thought he looked like death but had not realized he was actually dying and on his deathbed. As sad as it is, I guess it is true when they say, "What goes around comes around."

I was fresh out of the hole for defending myself and placed in ICC's north wing GHI units. I immediately addressed my concerns about my DOR with staff. From the start, I was being ignored, given the run-around by all prison staff and counselors. No one seemed to care or wanted to help or listen to my story. I was innocent of this DOR, and I was not going to give up on the truth, on justice. I started the grievance processes, sending in a new grievance every day, addressing my side, the truth about my story. I felt beaten; months had passed with no real response. Just as I was about to give up, a contact monitor for Idaho's Department of Corrections came to see me. He questioned me, even listened to me and my story. A few weeks later, I was called into my case manager's office and informed that the DOR I had received for defending myself/fighting had been dismissed.

As it turns out, there was a videotape showing the entire altercation, proving what I was saying to be true. The truth came out; it just took finding the right person and it was my mother who found the gentleman that came to my rescue. ICC did not care about the truth; the truth was there were five staff members present, and not one noticed what had taken place. I could not believe the video was still available, that it had not been lost or destroyed. Unfortunately, during this time, I developed a bad case of depression. I only ate once a day and went months without saying a word to anyone. Why would I? Every time I spoke I felt like I was getting into trouble. Sadly, no one seemed to notice or care, which somehow pulled me into a deeper depression.

My spiraling depression made my time at ICC rough. There were times I did not go outside or see the light of day for months, nine months straight one time. And to add to my troubles, what happened in the west wing followed me to the north wing. I found myself with target on my back, a growing one. For months I was forced to defend myself over and over again. I am sure you have seen the movie *Shawshank Redemption,* where Andy had to defend himself from the sisters. Sometimes he was lucky enough to win a battle, and sometimes he was not so lucky. It was exactly what I went through.

In those times, I had no choice but to hide out in my cage (cell), waiting for the bruising and the swelling to subside enough before I could go to the chow hall. During these long, hard and brutal months, I lived in fear, not knowing when the next beatdown would come, wondering if the next could be my last. I was in this situation because prison staff would not, or could not, do their job. I came to the belief that I was a *nobody* in prison, that my life no longer mattered. Week after week, I was being beaten or robbed, and sometimes both (good times). I saw no way out; I felt there was nothing I could do. I tried to do what was right, only to have my face slammed to the concrete floor by prison staff. I believed my situation hopeless, that nothing could be worse than the life I was living, but was I ever wrong. It went from bad to worse after being raped.

Sadly I had grown used to the beat downs (the physical attacks), so when three men rushed into my cell, I tried to stand and defend myself as I usually did. I was immediately knocked to the floor and kicked. As I have said, sometimes you can fend them off, sometimes you can't. I thought they would leave after drawing blood, as they usually did, but two of the men held my upper body to the floor as the third pulled the scrubs from my lower body (ICC uses garments much like hospital gowns called scrubs instead of pants and shirts). I kicked furiously, only to be beaten into a state of consciousness wherein I was aware of what was going on around me, but my body was unable to move. What happened next is a blur, but I remember laughter as a sharp object was suddenly held to my neck, a prison shank. I fought as a man climbed on me, the two others beating me into a state of unconsciousness. I came to seconds later, struggling in pain under a sweaty man grunting on top of me, only to have a sharpened object pushed to my windpipe. The pain was unbearable, and I prayed for it to end, for him to just finish, and he did, striking me with his fist a couple more times before raising and joining his two laughing friends standing guard outside the cell door. I guess I was lucky; I did not suffer permanent brain damage, and his friends seemed uninterested in raping me.

I had once heard of a man being raped by his bunkie while in RDU. He was attacked in his sleep and had told others that there was nothing he could do, that his attacker was to powerful. I was told this young man approached officers explaining what had happened, only to be told if he wanted to go forward with his complaint that he would be taken to the hole while an investigation took place. The humiliated man refused to go forward, feeling he was being punished for his attack. As I heard this man's story, I thought there had to be more, that he must have somehow enticed his attacker. I also thought this was something that could never happen to me, that I would be able to fend off my attacker. Now I found myself in the exact same position as that young man.

As I've come to know, now rape is the most humiliating experience a human being can endure. It steals more than one's dignity, practically sucking the life from one's soul. Guilt and shame may walk hand and hand, and I definitely felt both emotions. But guilt is a feeling you have over something you have done, while shame is a feeling over who you are, and I was definitely more ashamed. Because of the shame involved, this is the first time I have ever spoken of what happened in that cell the day my humility was stolen.

After experiencing rape, I went into a complete mental and social isolation, a complete shutdown. I hid in my cage (my cell) not even coming out for meals. I was starving myself out of not only fear but from the shame and a total lack of confidence and humiliation. I began making weapons. I was no longer going to allow this madness to continue. I told myself that there will not be a next time. I was prepared to seriously hurt, to kill. I went without sleep, without nutrition. I was out of my mind, beyond madness. Then, as a beacon of light parting the darkness, I was called from my hell. I was told to pack my property (what was left and not stolen) that I was moving.

I was transported back to the yard (ISCI). The horror was over—no more being raped, beaten, and robbed. No more hiding, no more going without food. When I left ICC, I weighed hundred and twenty-two pounds. My time at ICC was a living nightmare; I hadn't seen or felt the sun on my face for nine months. There were times I didn't say a word to another human being for days, even months at a time. The sad thing is no one noticed or cared.

I have seen what years in prison can do to a man, how it changes thinking and behaviors. I have come to know all too well why many good souls give into suicide while in prison, and why prisons like Idaho have suicide watch programs. Inmates thought to be a suicide risk and/or inmates seeking help are often put on suicide watch, a program that places inmates in a solitary cell with no clothing or anything else one can hurt themselves with. An inmate worker watches over the at-risk inmate twenty-four hours a day to be sure they do not hurt or kill themselves while being held in seclusion. Unfortunately, it is a valuable and necessary program in a prison environment. Suicide attempts in prisons like Idaho have become more and more frequent, much more than the public is aware of. This information is often left unspoken of.

While in prison, individuals (inmates) like me are being raped, beaten, and robbed while doing the time they were sentenced to. In many cases, this leads to suicidal thoughts and, far too often, suicide itself. There are so many reasons why someone would consider suicide behind the walls. Family and financial problems become too much for many incarcerated. Others suffer from mental disorders like depression and schizophrenia that go untreated by prison medical staff. Drugs (overdose) and drug debt also play a part in suicide attempts while in prison (a twenty-four-year-old Idaho inmate overdosed and died in 2016 in an Idaho prison). Being discriminated against and bullied also plays a big role. And of course, there are the rapes and other physical abuses. Suicide attempts are so out of control that they have become the norm.

Prison officials and staff are often undertrained or have become hardened by the walls themselves. Many are unaware of how their actions affect the human beings in their care. Most individuals who are sent to prison are short-timers, only receiving a few years behind the walls. You would be surprised how many lives are destroyed in that short period. Destroying a life, taking away a family's future is not justice, it is a criminal act. All lives matter; a little kindness and compassion can go a long way (I am in no way speaking against the Black Lives Matter movement). I am so very grateful that I did not play into my own evil thought of suicide and become a statistic, a number on someone's piece of paper.

Prison is a place the young come and begin to mentally die as the old are physically forgotten! Wages for your sins are in prison years, at the expense of American families and taxpayers! They say once you walk through the gates of hell (prison's front gates), you must sell your soul to the devil if you want to survive. When conforming to the evils within the walls of a prison, this is very true. And once you have sold your soul, you become institutionalized and serve no good to anyone, including yourself.

Prison life is hard in itself. Being hardheaded can make it harder, but being naïve can make it nearly impossible. I am sure you have heard the phrase "Don't burn any bridges along the way; you may need them on your way back." What I am saying is, from the day you are arrested to the time you are released, do not piss on or piss off anyone because that person may be your bunkie and/or your cellmate someday. During my journey through the system, I came across individuals I had meet early on in my nightmare, only to be housed with them toward the end. Lucky for me, I keep my mouth shut and was respectful no matter what. I am a small man; my average weight is about one hundred fifty pounds. On a good day, with thick soles on my shoes, I stand five feet, seven inches tall. For someone like me, it is wiser to be smarter than the stocking bullies.

I knew a guy who was always on the punk list (the target list). Like me, he was small, but he was no coward. He was tired of being punked out all the time (beat and stolen from), and he took his revenge in a most unusual way. For months he snuck around leaving his excrement (his shit) on bunks of those who picked on him. No one knew who was doing it, and those who heard of this started calling this young man the Mad Pooper, or Poop Houdini. I'm just saying, if you piss off someone in prison, you may want to check under your pillow before you lay your head down. For months, this was an out-of-control situation; this guy could have been killed. I do respect his courage but feel it was not worth risking his life over. Lucky for him, he was never caught.

Idaho's prisons are in a state of constant change. The prison population is getting crazier; new mentality is coming into play. While doing my time and research, I have come across one madness after another. For many of the younger men, going to prison is a badge of honor. They think doing time behind the walls makes them a man, someone who deserves respect. They think it is cool to be in prison, and this is where the prison bucket list (must-do list) comes into play.

This is a type of bragging rights among their so-called friends, where stories of greatness are told, the "My dad is tougher than your dad" contest of junior high school.

While doing my time, I have come to know of the troubling mentality of the young prison inmates, and the majority of the younger men do have a prison bucket list, the must-do list, here in Idaho prisons. All seem to want a prison tattoo (unfortunately, most of these kids were not smart enough to comprehend the dangers of this—contracting hepatitis C, MRSA, and/or AIDS from unsterile tattoo equipment). Many want to join prison gangs and beat sex offenders and/or rats (someone who is accused of telling). Many brag of smuggling contraband in their rectum, extorting the weak for commissary, and stealing from others. Others brag of having sex with, or in some cases, raping a transgender or confused young man. Sex with prison staff or having them bring in contraband such as drugs or cell phones are the medal of valor, the ultimate badge of honor. In every prison facility across the state of Idaho, this is the general consensus of a majority of the prison inmate population.

For years, Idaho has sent inmates to prisons for profit in other states (private prisons). Most of these Idaho inmates were being housed at other CCA facilities throughout the country, the same corporation that had a finical relationship with Idaho's Governor Otter. There is an old saying, "If it quacks like a duck, looks like a duck, and acts like a duck, it must be a duck." And there is only one word for this cozy finical relationship: *corruption*. There was more money to be made this way for Idaho's elite politicians and its prison for profit partner, CCA. This corruption was also much deeper than it appeared, obviously.

As part of the contract, CCA agreed to supply every Idaho inmate with a job paying eighty dollars a month. However, nearly all these so-called jobs were not jobs at all. In other words, Idaho inmates were bribed; they were paid off by the state. This without saying is manipulation, deception, and fraud, and yes, it a form of corruption. Inmates housed out of state also repeatedly failed drug testing. This was curved by testing the same inmates, inmates that could pass a drug test week after week. The underpaid staff were often caught with contraband; one woman was found with fourteen cell phones in her possession. There were cases of pregnancies and other signs of chaos left unchecked. One Idaho inmate was beaten to death in Oklahoma and lay in his bunk for two days before guards noticed. There is something wrong with this entire picture, this practice of sending inmates convicted of crimes against Idaho to other states to do their time.

At some point, all those inmates had to come back to Idaho prisons. That is the ones that did not top their sentences out of state; they were simply released in the state they were held whether they had resources to live there or not. In 2016, all Idaho's out-of-state inmates were brought back to Idaho, but this chapter in Idaho's prison history is not quite closed. For the last twenty-or-so years that Idaho inmates were coming and going from out of state prisons for profit, they brought back to Idaho a whole new level of prison mentality, things Idaho had never seen or dealt with, and Idaho is still feeling the repercussions. Gangs and gang violence is on the rise, and violent acts have skyrocketed since bringing inmates back. Manipulation and compromising of prison staff has also become a big problem for Idaho prisons. Idaho's prisons have changed and not in a good way, all because someone, somewhere was more interested in making money, then having Idaho's and its citizens best interest at heart.

In all my years in prison, the Idaho prison system has always done its banking with a local bank here in Boise, Idaho (Syringa Bank). Though I have heard stories of those who have, I for one have never had a problem with my inmate account. I will be honest; I am not sure if it was a good system for the Idaho inmate, but it was a system that worked well. However, as of July 1, 2016, Idaho's prison banking system began a change, sending Idaho's money and its business out of Idaho to a bank in St. Louis, Missouri. Now it costs Idaho citizens to deposit money in to inmate's accounts, depending on the amount deposit, ranging from two dollars and ninety-five cents up to ten dollars and ninety-five cents per deposit. There was never a fee to deposit money in an inmate's account prior to this banking change. Again, I must question why Idaho's Department of Corrections stopped using a local ran bank and is now doing its banking business out of Idaho.

Though I am not an economist and have no specific facts, it is obvious the answer is greed. I do not know the exact numbers, but it is also obvious that the Idaho Department of Corrections inmate trust account is a very large account. I am guessing well over two hundred and fifty thousand (probably more) at any given time. If each inmate in Idaho only had one dollar a week in their account, it would add up to over five thousand dollars a week, twenty thousand a month, eighty thousand a quarter. I realize that many inmates do not have any money, but many more have much more than a dollar. And if you figure in the expensive, one-time property purchases such as televisions, you will see that two hundred and fifty thousand is a very conservative figure. It would only make sense that the commissary vendor, Keefe Commissary, is paid quarterly and that there is a great deal of interest to be paid on such an account. I am guessing an account that large could easily gain five percent interest, adding to a conservative figure of twelve thousand five hundred a year (I am sure it is much more).

Many would think that this is simply good economics, but that money or the compounding interest does not belong to the Idaho Department of Corrections; it belongs to the inmates and the inmates families. And even more troubling is how and where that money is going. The money is actually supposed to be put in an inmate trust account and spent on the inmates themselves but never is. I for one would like to see the records of this inmate account, see who exactly is in charge of that money and where is it spent. Why is it not spent on education, job training, or release funds?

While in prison, I was subject to many troubling situations; it is what it is once assigned a state issued number. One has to endure nudity and the reek of men passing gas or defecating nearby. Inmates are often strip-searched next to one another; I know I have seen more than my share of penises. There are a lot of jerks, loudmouths, a-holes, tought guys and bullies. Do you know what they all got in common besides shit-talking and storytelling? They all use their size and weight to compensate for having small wee wees, you know little dicks. And one would think by the stories told that the Idaho prison is full of South American drug lords. I have heard every "I got this," "I got that," "I used to be one of the biggest drug dealers in America" story I can stomach. Then you will see each of these storytellers going around every morning begging for a cup of coffee because they are flat broke, yet they have a Lamborghini at home and a playboy bunny as a wife.

I was also subjected to all kinds of varying personalities while doing my time. Everybody wants to be a *somebody*. It seems every idiot in prison wants to be a rapper, a high roller, a baller, an MMA fighter, or a player like Hugh Hefner of *Playboy* magazine. Heads up to all those inmates—you will never be like Hugh Hefner; he had to work to become what he is today. He is in a class all by himself, period, so stop trying. Many inspire to be a *gangster*. Fact—listen up, all you wannabe gangsters, keep thinking you want to be a gangster and your future will be prison for life or, worse yet, death. There is no future in being a so-called gangster. Funny thing, during my research, I asked around the prison talking to the younger inmates, and 99 percent of them said they were gangsters. Every time I asked if they wanted to be like Al Capone, most said yes (the ones that actually knew who Al Capone was anyway). I wonder if they would say that if they knew he spent most of his life in prisons like Alcatraz and then died a lonely and painful death from syphilis. The ones I explained this to still inspired to be a gangster. The majority of young prison inmates, from what I have experienced, are undereducated. The national grade average of education for prisoners in the United States is the eleventh grade; I am sure Idaho's average is much lower. But I guess that would make sense when considering Idaho has one of the highest high school dropout rates in the nation.

As I mentioned earlier in this chapter, Idaho pays inmates to help watch at-risk inmates, to help prevent inmates from committing suicide (suicide watch program). Idaho prisons also pay inmates to help the handicapped, pushing inmates confined to wheelchairs to the chow hall and other appointments. Idaho prisons are filled with handicapped inmates, and there are a lot of them, hundreds. The majority should not be in prison, and most go without proper treatment for their needs. These wheelchair pushers are the lifeline to the individual who is handicapped; many pushers also help in feeding and bathing the man they have been entrusted with. Without this service, handicapped inmates would not survive in prison. Though I been violently raped, beaten, and robbed, I for one have never had a medical emergency while in prison. I have managed and dealt with my injuries on my own. There were a few times I needed medical attention, but I knew if I brought that kind of attention on myself, my future would be short. Your emergency is not the prison's emergency. From what I have seen, serious medical emergencies in prison end up in an inmate's death. Medical response time takes forever, and if outside medical attention is needed, it can take an ambulance hours to get past the red tape and pass through security at the front gates. And again, inmates with a serious conditions end up in death.

My last few years in prison, I had a serious problem with rodents (mice and rats) getting in my locker and storage boxes, consuming my overly priced commissary food items. I was not the only one who was having a rodent problem. I learned that the prison had killed off the feral cats living on and running around the prison grounds. After doing so, the rodents took over.

Many inmates watched over these feral cats, claiming they brought a little piece of sanity into their bleak world. I also found out that guards had shot and killed a fox that had somehow found its way onto the prison grounds. Inmates loved this fox, but it was callously exterminated. Many inmates also feed the birds that come around, and I have found out that prison staff has been setting mouse traps for the sparrows. Other local wildlife in the area have been killed as well. Besides the killing of the cats, the prison has also killed rabbits, gofers, whistle-pigs, snakes (harmless ones) ground squirrels, and other birds such as owls, killdeers and seagulls. On October 12, 2016, I walked the prison grounds and counted sixty-three poison traps on the prison grounds. And yet there has been nothing done about the rodent problems in the housing unit I was living in. All my life I've never had a rodent problem in my home or in my living area, not until I came to an Idaho prison. And on another disturbing tale of animal cruelty, Idaho's Maximum Security Institution (IMSI) and

Idaho's State Correctional Institution (ISCI) are the only two prison facilities in Idaho that use dogs as security. Many times I've witness these helpless animals being kicked, being mistreated by prison staff.

These animals are subjected to the outside elements all year around, no matter if it's below freezing or over hundred degrees outside. These poor animals are doing for worst time than I. It's truly is a sad situation for these animals.

Since the killing of these animals by the use of traps and poisons, the prison has paid inmates to not only set traps for sparrows but to stomp and beat rodents and whistle-pigs with shovels. I have watched these inmates at work, and I truly believe they enjoy their work far too much. The gist of what I am trying to say is that the prison has killed off the animals that bring peace to the minds of inmates and allowed troubled inmates to callously kill wildlife in a way that would be considered animal cruelty. Does that make any sense to you?

Not everyone in prison is a criminal, nor do all incarcerated deserve a second chance. Nevertheless, the majority of inmates have been sentenced to exceedingly long sentences for low-level crimes such as possession of narcotics (drugs) and DUIs. Most belong in treatment facility centers and do not belong or deserve to be incarcerated for multiple years with little or no treatment at the expense of tax payers. I might remind you that our last three presidents have admitted to smoking marijuana, and George W Bush received treatment for alcoholism. And as I have mentioned before, several of Idaho's leaders have been arrested, charged, and convicted of more than just alcohol-related crimes (Butch Otter, Mike Crapo, Larry Craig, Mike Magee, and John Bujak, to name a few), all of which say they made a mistake and have been given a second chance (some a third and even a fourth). My point is, if the leaders of the free world can openly admit to smoking marijuana and alcoholism and state leaders as the ones I mentioned above can be convicted of crimes and given second chances, than why shouldn't the citizens they are working for be awarded the same opportunity?

Idaho prisons do have treatment programs inside, but these programs are forced on the inmate undermining their effectiveness (do the program or don't get out). Most inmates consider them a joke, a way for Idaho to suck money from the federal government. Inmates are forced to tell on one another, frequently putting that inmate's safety at risk (I have mentioned the video of the violent beating of an inmate in an Idaho program). Inmates are also subjected to degrading role playing, imitating homosexual activity, sucking on an invisible popsicle, licking invisible ice-cream cones, acting as valley girls breaking up with a boyfriend, scooting across the floor like a dog with worms, etc. The idea was to break down stereotypes and personas portrayed by inmates. However, though they may work for some, these role plays have had an adverse effect on many. Idaho has done away with some of their programming, replacing most with a Cincinnati, Ohio, model. The word among inmates is that little has actually changed other than the name.

Unfortunately in today's world jails and prisons are absolutely needed, but America's ridicules policies of mass incarceration is destroying the very youth they claim to protect and a complete waste of taxpayer dollars. When prisons become a business for profit, it undermines justice, and that is what should be considered a true crime against humanity. I must ask, is America the greatest country in the world? Our policies and actions against your own brothers and sisters say otherwise; we must do better!

CHAPTER 7

Living with a Killer

I have been housed in five separate institutions within the state of Idaho's prison system. The Yard (ISCI); Idaho's former private prison, ICC (now called ISCC since the state takeover); the Farm (SICI), Orofino (NICI) and the Nampa Community Release Center (CRC). Each has subtle differences in operation, creating a personality of their own. There are constant power outages, toxic water outbreaks, and both plumbing and sewage problems (toilets backing up with fecal matter). Each one was a living nightmare in itself, each leaving my soul forever scarred.

Being designated as the property of Idaho and not a citizen or even a person, I was often subjected to cruel and unusual living environments. I have spent years housed in a warehouse (a tool shed at best) with little heat, and forced to sleep throughout the winter months wearing every piece of clothing I had (I have been told that there were actually skiffs of ice in the toilets of ISCI's eight house in December of 2001). I have been held in cages (cells) with windows that did not close or were completely broken out, leaving me as well as others exposed to the outside elements, not to mention the flies and other insects. I have been forced to live amongst asbestos made materials that were completely covered in lead base paints. And I have lived in housing units that felt as sweat lodges during the summer months. If one complains, they often hear the usual speech given by staff, "If you don't like it, then don't come to prison." "Yeah, I get it and I do realize it is prison."

Living in a prison environment is not easy for anyone, but it can become especially hard when forced to live with psychopaths who are killers, and at times, can even become life-threatening. Being state property, you do as you are told, and you eat, sleep, and live where assigned. An argument with prison staff can and often will send you to the Hole (solitary confinement as a disciplinary action). Throughout Idaho's prison system, there is no real segregation; rapist and murders roam freely among first-time drug offenders. That is just the way the ball rolls around here; if you don't like it, refer back to the guard's speech: don't come to prison.

During my years in prison, I have had all types of cellmates, ranging from the mentally challenged (congenitally below-average intelligence) to gifted geniuses that one would never expect to find in an institution. I have lived with people with extreme physical abilities as well as those with severe physical disabilities. Mental health funding across the United Sates has been cut to a bare minimum, forcing police and the justice system to deal with those suffering with mental disabilities. Too often, states such as Idaho have no answer to this growing problem, and both the mentally and physically disabled end up with prison number and serving a prison sentence. I had one cellmate with such severe mental disabilities that he had no idea where he was, nor did he understand he was in a prison (no clue). I have also been forced to live in a cell with individuals who suffered with severe paranoia, a terrible situation to find yourself in.

Schizophrenia and violence seem to walk hand and hand. One kid I was forced to live with was so out there, way out there, that he literally thought he was the Hulk, consistently trying to smash me. This made life a living hell while in that cell. I also lived in a cell with a cannibal (a person who likes to eat human flesh)—of course, this made me a little paranoid. I once had a deaf and mute cellmate who could not talk (communicate) or hear anything. You would think this would be an ideal cellmate for someone as reclusive as me, but he refused to shower and began to stink so bad that staff had to wash him down with a fire hose every other week. I was forced to live with many inmates with life-threatening diseases or conditions such as AIDS, Hepatitis C, MRSA, and every kind of sexually transmitted disease (STD) known to man.

I have experienced every type of prison living condition there is while doing my time in Idaho and have concluded that dorm living is the most disgusting environment of all. Dorms are often overcrowded and noisy. There is no respect whatsoever; individuals will uncaringly urinate, even defecate on the floors. All Idaho prison facilities lack in bathroom amenities, thus making life rough when suffering from the diarrhea you developed after eating the fine prison cuisine. It is not uncommon for at least one toilet to be out of order, creating long waits. Showers are always disgustingly dirty, and men are constantly caught having sex with one another inside of them. Many men behind the walls (maybe even a majority) shave their entire bodies, leaving sink and shower drains continuously clogged with mounds of men's pubic and body hair.

The noise is constant. Men defecate nearby or lie beside you, wallowing in the reek of their own gas; believe me, it's overwhelming on your senses. Imagine sharing one toilet with twenty-five individuals who are, for the most part, neither clean nor healthy, having some type of sores and/or blisters covering their bodies and continually bleeding. And let's not forget about the dirt bags that leave not just their saliva but their snot (nasal mucus) and boogers on everything they touch— floors, walls, etc. A majority of the people stink because of their state-issued clothing. Prison laundry is only available twice a week, leaving you to wear dirty, stinky underwear, socks, and other clothing five days a week. Some individuals adapt and wash their own clothing in buckets, sinks, and even toilets. Yes, I said they wash their clothes in the same toilet they shit in, but others simply do not seem to care (or are too heavily medicated) and will miss laundry two or three weeks in a row.

Living conditions are slightly better in cells. Most cells only hold two people, though there are some single cells available for inmate workers working prison jobs. However, what makes or breaks cell life is the bunkie you are assigned to live with. I am sure all are aware it can be difficult to get along with people at times; especially with those individuals who struggle with mental health issues. These individuals are more likely to have violent tendencies, that can create an explosive situation for anyone who is locked in a cage with them.

I for one have low points (a low custody classification). I am also a short-timer (someone with a short sentence or little time left on their sentence) and have no institutional disciplinary history (a clean history). Yet I have been forced to live with people convicted of multiple homicides in my prison career. I found myself being housed with cold-blooded killers doing life without the possibility of parole. The first killer I lived with was a young kid who had stabbed another kid in the chest twenty-six times (an overkill I would say). He bragged about it, stating he enjoyed the power he felt during the killing, that he enjoyed feeling the young man's soul leaving his body. Another guy, a military man, committed a double homicide, killing his ex-girlfriend and her lover. He was extremely intelligent, and that scared me even more than the other man. He was manipulative and evil, having a Hannibal Lector type intelligence. Another cold-blooded killer I was forced to live with shot a stranger in the face and bragged of blowing the man's face completely off. But it was the last one I lived with that was the most frightening, paling the others. He was psychotic, a psychopathic killer who had no respect for human life. He was doing life for cutting another man's throat.

One day, during the afternoon count (four o'clock), he came into our cell looking for something. I was not paying much attention to him because I had learned what he did was none of my business. About ten minutes into his search, he began getting frustrated and then grew irate and started swearing about a honey bun (an overly priced frosted cinnamon roll). Again, I was just minding my own business as he was going about his. He suddenly stopped his frantic search and glared directly at me, asking what I had done with his honey bun with a sour voice. I was startled by his question, but more so by his attitude and body posture. Trying calmly as I could, I simply said, "How would I know?"

By this time he was boiling, steaming from head to toe. Once again he looked at me, this time saying, "I have killed once before, I can kill again." I was confused, even shocked by his words, but did not want to look weak (probably a mistake on my part). I jumped up, confronting him on the death threat he just made towards me. Just as I was up, this nut ball attacked me and we ended up in a fight. Being locked in a cell (cage), there is no place to go or hide; it is like being in an octagon cage match, MMA style, but without a referee. The fight did not last long, neither of us hurting the other much. Looking back, I consider myself lucky; the man really had killed before. I mean, what are they going to do to someone already doing life? A short time later, he found his honey bun, but unfortunately, our relationship was already over. He had accused me of taking his honey bun, threatened my life, and attacked me.

Later that night while I was lying on my bunk, he attacked me again, but this time he had a weapon, a prison shank. I had been poked and cut during his initial attack that night. My hand and wrist were bleeding, but I managed to overpower him, wrenching the weapon from his hand. I am sure God must have been watching over me that day.

I stayed in that cell for three long days (and longer nights) afterwards. For three days I went without sleep, until the third day when I finally went to staff pleading to be removed before someone (probably me) was killed. I was not questioned, nor were there any problems with prison staff about my request, a relieving surprise that made me very grateful. This psychotic psychopath wanted to kill me over an eighty-five-cent honey bun. I was not about to lose my life over a honey bun, but then again, I should not have been in the same cell with a person who was doing life for murder. I was mentally changed by this experience, disturbed. I lay awake and thought about this experience for weeks afterwards. I nearly fell into the evil ways of prison; I could have lost my life over an eighty-five-cent honey bun. I am still not fully recovered from this experience (it is what it is), but I believe I can and will be, for I truly believe God is on my side.

In conclusion to living with a killer, I'm sorry to say an inmate who was serving a short prison sentence for a DUI offense was beaten to death in a cell by his cellmate. Who by the way was doing life without parole for killing multiple people (his family). This killing took place on the yard (ISCI) in eleven house in September 2017.

CHAPTER 8

Being in the Danger Zone
Violence behind the Walls

A violent act can occur anywhere, to anyone, at any given moment behind the walls. No one is safe within the confinement of a prison, no one. As I have informed you in earlier chapters, I have suffered my share of black eyes, fat lips, and bruising. I have felt the calloused tip of a real prison shank pushed to my windpipe and endured the pain of a crude and uncaring blade as it ripped and cut into my flesh, scarring my hand and wrist area. Though I have been the target of attack after attack, I feel blessed; most individuals are left permanently disfigured or do not survive such brutality. Some choose to end the nightmares and pain by their own hands, cutting their own wrist or hanging themselves.

I cannot begin to estimate the amount of abuse I have endured, the number of beatings I have lived through, the number of times I have considered taking my own life while serving my time in Idaho's county jails and prisons. The attacks I suffered, the beatings, the robberies, even the rape have become a tangled chaotic blur. If I were to guess at the staggering number of attacks inflicted upon me, the estimate would be in the neighborhood of fifty, maybe more. Even one is too many. No one should be subjected to even one such brutal attack, and unfortunately, I have witnessed ten times the amount inflicted upon me, with only a handful actually reported and dealt with by jail or prison staff.

There are overwhelming numbers of unreported acts of violence behind the walls. Possibly as high as 90 percent go unreported, an astounding number. Jail and prison staff have a large role in the violence being inflicted. Many staff members will turn their heads, allowing the violence to continue and even escalate because of additional effort and paperwork that may be required from them. Some even enjoy the violence or believe sex offenders and inmates considered troublemakers deserve to be beaten. I personally believe no human being deserves to be treated inhumanely. Nationally, there were 1.2 million violent crimes reported to the FBI by police departments across the country in 2012. In that same year there were a little more than 5.8 million violent crimes reported by prisoners while incarcerated in a jail or prison. Although these numbers are far less from the truth.

During my stay in the Ada county jail, I was forced to defend myself three times; not one of them was reported to staff. I could not report these incidents because officers would do little or nothing it would put me at greater risk of continued attacks. While working in the Ada county jail's kitchen, there is a saying when having a problem with someone: "Freezer up!" There are no working cameras in the freezer, and this is often where the real cage fighting takes place. Obviously, jail staff is aware of this activity, yet the cage fighting continues. Most of the violence I have witnessed could have been prevented if jail staff were actually doing the job they are being paid to do. It is also obvious that most of the jail staff simply do not care or are too lazy to do anything about it. I also know that some not only enjoy the violence but display violent tendencies and abuse inmates themselves.

Ada county jail is out of control with violence. This is simply unacceptable! Young men are living in fear while county-paid sheriff deputies are too busy on their smart phones, paying little or no attention to the safety of the human beings entrusted in their care and depending on them while in jail.

In prison, you are always in the danger zone; no one is safe. Besides the obvious reasons such as gambling, gambling debts, and drugs, a violent act can also suddenly erupt when one's pride is hurt, out of feelings of being disrespected over sports, politics, or religion: even farting in the shower can get you knocked out. This one time while I was in the shower area, I watched a guy get knocked out, and before he hit the ground, he shit himself; it made me throw up. Prison violence can also surface from simple boredom, inmates beating a weaker inmate just because they can. Stepping on someone's shoes can get you hurt. Dayroom televisions are also a source of many fights (it's all about the control). Horseplay between friends can get ugly real quick. Hate, discrimination, and racism play a major role in prison violence (especially in Idaho's system, where there is no segregation between higher and lower level offenders whatsoever). Not washing your hands after the use of the bathroom can give you a real headache up against a concrete wall. Greed and jealousy play a role; fear and anxiety do not help in the cause. Many Idaho's prison inmates have front teeth missing due to some type of prison violence, and I have seen my share of them being kicked or knocked out. I've seen many teeth being spit out, rolling on the ground like dice on a craps table. So far I'm lucky; I still have mine.

Idaho is infamous for having one of the country's most violent prisons, ISCC (the old ICC). To be honest, that is nothing too be proud of. It is an outrage, a total disgrace to the good citizens of Idaho. We as Americans are not naïve; I am sure most of us believe prison is and always will be a dangerous and violent place, but how does a 2,500-bed facility in a state with a young prison population and little racial divide get such a violent reputation? And more importantly, why do we believe prisons are and always will be violent? I am asking why is this acceptable. Why do prison institutions have to be viewed and accepted in such a way?

A great deal of prison violence has to do with food, or the lack of food. Besides the fact that prisoners have had everything else taken away, food turns into a luxury, there is also the fact that many inmates are underfed. At times, it looks as if we live in a third-world nation. I have actually witnessed on many occasions men digging food out of the garbage because they are hungry.

Here's an example of the point I am trying to make. I am a small guy, on average about 150 pounds. I live with a man who is 6'7" and weighs 275 pounds. He is a big guy who is always cranky because he is always hungry. We both get the same amount of food each day, and I know a lot of you are thinking that it is only fair everyone receives the same amount each day, but is it? Now let me give another example. Let's say I have a Honda Civic, and I put five dollars' worth of gas in the tank. My bunkie drives a Hummer and he also puts the same amount of gas in his tank (five dollars). We both leave the gas station at the same time and are traveling at the same speed, but who do you believe will run out of gas first, me or my bunkie? Obviously my bunkie will run out of fuel before I do and will go hungry sooner. When big men in prison go hungry, it puts small guys like me in an unsafe environment.

I have also wondered about the water system. All the water on Idaho's prison row is ground water pumped from onsite wells. ISCC (the former ICC) has their own well while the rest of the state run facilities share a well. I am unsure where the private prison owned by MTC (Idaho's CAPP program facility) obtains its water supply. There is also a waste water treatment pond onsite, along with ranches, farms, and the nearby wild horse corrals.

In 2010, ICC had an outbreak of *E. coli*, in which the Idaho National Guard was called to bring in water until the system could be flushed. They had another outbreak in 2011. The water tower for the rest of the state-owned facilities was also contaminated with dead birds about that same time and also had to be flushed and cleaned. Many water systems in eastern Idaho have naturally occurring cyanide in the water. Many inmates sent to the St. Anthony work camps are given the opportunity to work in potato warehouses with signs warning of drinking the water, but inmates have no other available water source. I recently asked a staff member (Mr. Ward) at ISCI about the water and was told during training that officers and other IDOC staff were advised not to drink the water in any of the prison row facilities. With that being said why is it okay for inmates to drink the water and not okay for those who are in control. Are we not the same? I'm no water expert, but the color of the water throughout Idaho's infamous prison row facilities is not normal water color as being clear. There is a tint of yellow, gray, and light brown in color at times, not always but most of the time. Obviously, there is something wrong with the water on prison row for IDOC to tell its own employees not to drink it. This leads me to wonder if the water supply has anything to do with the violence on prison row.

I truly feel that sweeping, common sense changes made throughout America's prison system would greatly reduce prison population, rate of recidivism, and the untold amounts of violence behind the walls. First of all, it must start with jail and prison staff doing the job in which the taxpayers are paying them to do (simple enough, right). Respect goes both ways, and a little of it can make a big difference in the lives of both the incarcerated and the staff entrusted with watching over them. Mistakes are made, but neglectful and/or abusive staff must be held accountable.

Not everyone within the walls of a jail or a prison are incorrigible or irredeemable (mistakes are made). Compassion, courtesy, and kindness can go a long way for someone who is down on hope. Understanding the suffering of others and grasping the fact that all people make mistakes can make a real difference in the lives of not only those imprisoned but will often make prison and jail staff's jobs easier and more enjoyable. Respect does go both ways.

Education and job training are also at the top of the must-change list. Many inmates are repeat offenders who have little or no job skills and feel they have nothing to look forward to in life beyond the walls. I compared our justice system to the segregation system known as the Jim Crow System of the 1870s (chapter 4). In that system, the wealthy separatists knew they could keep control of freed slaves by keeping them uneducated, which in return kept them in poverty with little or no hope of advancing. They were also able to keep better control of the poor white population by making them feel superior to the undereducated and poor former slaves.

Therefore, by not educating the young prison population, by not giving them the skills and job training needed to make a real change in their lives, the American prison system is segregating our young and poor in the same way the Jim Crow System of America's past had. We, as Americans, are allowing a separation in classes to the likes never seen since the Jim Crow era. I have heard it said that insanity is doing the same things over and over and expecting different results. If that is a true definition of insanity, then America's prison system is truly insane.

Inmate segregation within the walls would make a huge difference in curving and controlling prison violence, but I am not talking about racial segregation. Individuals who are doing life without parole do not have the same outlook on life as a short-timer. I have seen the ugly truth and almost lost my life because of it. Inmates with long sentences for violent crimes should be separated from nonviolent offenders. Anyone convicted of capital crimes such as murder should be housed at Idaho's Maximum Security Institution, at least for the first few years of their sentence, and should not be allowed in lower-level institutions until they are within ten years of release (five years of release for work programs) and have proven themselves by their institutional behavior (must be free of disciplinary violations). However, I am in no way suggesting these inmates be caged as animals with no hope. The warden at Idaho's IMSI recently stated in a television interview that when inmates are treated as animals, that is how they act once returned to society. I agree with this statement and am merely suggesting separating violent inmates from those convicted of nonviolent crimes until they have proven they have curved their aggressive tendencies.

Nevertheless, I believe that lower-custody-level inmates (as well as the more aggressive after a period of time) should be allowed to work their way into better living conditions and opportunities by proving themselves with their behavior. I believe inmates truly wishing to better their lives through education and job training will not jeopardize such opportunities with foolish behavior.

For example, Idaho has four main housing facilities on prison row. One, is Idaho State Correctional Center (ISCC) aka gladiator school. Two, is Idaho Maximum Security Institution (IMSI) aka MAX. Third, is South Idaho Correctional Institution (SICI) aka the

Farm. And the fourth, is Idaho State Correctional Institution (ISCI) aka the yard. Very few inmates want to do their time at ISCC's (gladiator school) so this is where all inmates should start their time. Inmates should work their way out of ISCC and into other facilities with good behavior and be allowed the opportunity of education, job training, and good time (time off their sentences for good behavior). From there they should be sent to work camps and community work release centers. Also, as an inmate progresses through the education and job training process (from one institution to another), they should be rewarded with better meals, living conditions, and more freedom such as conjugal visits, and at least a one day pass a month from work centers (a pass that would allow inmates to do their banking, search for housing, buy clothing, and visit with family). I say to you, inmates who have such opportunities will not jeopardize losing earned goodtime and freedom worked for. I am not saying all will conform or even comply, but I am saying the numbers that do conform would be staggering with unheard success rates and it would save a boat load of tax dollars each and every year.

I realize many reading this may believe I am speaking of turning prisons into college campuses, but this is far from what I am talking about. Separating individuals convicted of crimes from society is the punishment and retribution for committing those crimes. Prison sentences are also meant as a deterrent, a warning to those who may commit a crime. The idea is to protect the general public, but how is our society protected by locking a human being in a dangerous and hostile environment for years and then returning them into that very society with a lowered expectation and outlook on civilization and humanity, as well as life itself? Remember the words of the US temperance campaigner, Carry Nation (1846–1911): "You have put me in here a cub, but I will come out roaring like a lion, and I will make all hell howl!" I hope I am howling in a positive way, but the sad truth is, most who have been treated as animals during incarceration do not howl in such a positive way once returned to society. And as for the deterrent aspect, if that really worked, then there would never be a need to build another prison because everyone would be detoured already.

Many may believe the financial burden would be overwhelming, and in no way could society afford such programs. I say to those that it would be more cost-effective in the long run. Inmates working in work camps and community work centers could actually generate the money needed to pay for such programs. This is a proven fact. Inmates are already charged 30 percent of their income before taxes in Idaho's four community work centers (three for men and one for women). What I am suggesting is increasing the number of work centers. I propose every incarcerated inmate be afforded the opportunity to not only find a job, but locate housing, obtain clothing, a driver licenses, and other necessities needed to be successful upon release. Besides saving states hundreds of thousands of dollars in future incarceration cost per inmates returning to prison, states would also financially benefit from future tax dollars generated from people who, under the current prison system, would remain or be returned to incarceration. And let's not forget the amount of revenue that states would gather in fines and restitution that under the current system would go unpaid.

Many may believe that I am suggesting individuals convicted of a crime should be afforded a greater opportunity for education and job training than the children of poor and struggling families across America. This also could not be further from the truth. What I am suggesting is prison reform. I agree that there is a need for reform in education and job training beyond the walls. However, what I am suggesting would in no way give those incarcerated an advantage over those who are not. As mentioned above, inmates benefiting from these programs would bear the burden of the cost.

In conclusion, what I am suggesting is compressive reform to curve prison recidivism and violence. I have seen the ugly truth, experienced the violence firsthand, and almost lost my life because of it. I know firsthand of how America has become a nation of incarceration at the cost of the very citizens the prison system is supposed to be protecting. This madness is costing taxpayers billions of dollars while a handful of politicians spew frightening propaganda to create a separation in classes for personal gain, to reap the benefits of incarcerating you or your children. America cannot afford to continue on this destructive path. The current prison system is a breeding ground for violence, turning the young who have made a mistake into hardened criminals. Why must we believe prisons are and always will be violent? Why is this acceptable, why must penal institutions be viewed and accepted in such a way?

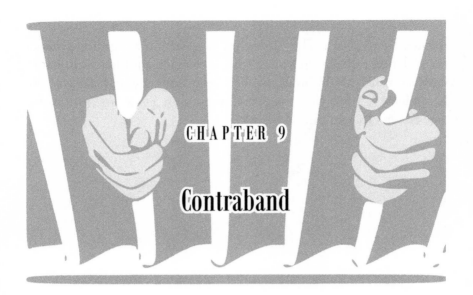

CHAPTER 9

Contraband

What is *contraband*? It is usually some type of smuggled goods, something prohibited inside prison institutions, such as drugs, tobacco, or pornography. However, it is anything and everything prison officials say contraband is. Contraband can be an altered pair of sunglasses or a worn pair of gym shorts purchased from the prison commissary store, or even a piece of fruit that was given to you by the prison for your lunch. But the two most common are tobacco and illegal drugs.

The very first time I saw drugs behind the walls was in the Ada county jail. There was so much of it (mostly methamphetamine) that I was actually shocked to the point of disgust. I question why and how drugs could run wild in a jail. I stopped my questioning after arriving in the Idaho State Prison and finding drugs and drug use running rampant in Idaho's prison institutions.

My first time in prison (through the gates of despair), within the first few hours of my arrival, I was exposed to the truth when walking into my assigned cell and finding an inmate (my bunkie) with a needle in his arm. Unfortunately, since then, I have seen dozens of inmates doing the same thing. I have found needles in trash cans, seen empty baggies and used needles on the ground while out and about the prison grounds. Once, while walking the prison grounds, I found a bag of methamphetamine the size of a golf ball. I admit thoughts rolled in my mind a fleeting moment, but I was able to chase those momentary thoughts away and flee as quickly as possible. I am not claiming to be an angel; I have self-medicated in the past and admit I was very tempted. But one thing being in prison has taught me, it's best to walk away, because if anyone knew I had their drugs, I could have been killed or have been a victim of future beatings and or become a target of extortion. Not to mention being charged with possession and introducing contraband (to wit, narcotics) into a state facility.

During my incarceration, I have seen firsthand the ugly truth of how drug use leads to addiction and addiction leads to violence. A huge number of prison inmates are caught up in this vicious cycle, in this madness. Drug use in prison is out of control; people are dying (the last known overdose that I know of was on August 3, 2016, in eleven-house on the yard, ISCI). People are getting themselves hurt and beaten to pay drug debts and/or are forced to engage in sexual acts.

Prison drug dealers promote their product on Inmate dot-com (by-word-of mouth advertising) and by giving a select few free samples of what they have. Drugs on the inside cost four or five times what they might on the out (no wonder it leads to huge debts and problems behind the walls). Sadly, most drugs are handed out at medical, medication prescribed to inmates, and smuggled back to be sold for commissary items such as coffee or stamped envelopes (Idaho has one of the highest medicated prison population in the nation). Food is gold; sometimes I think there is less food in prison than there are drugs. Commissary items (food, coffee, and envelopes) will get you any drug you need or want.

While in prison, I'm forced to live with paranoid, out-of-control drug addicts who keep me up at nights. People who may or may not have self-medicated in the past are turned into addicts on the inside, learning to hustle and steal to pay for their short-lived escapes from the harsh reality of prison, acquiring newly formed habits. When addicts reach this point, no one is safe from their madness.

I can only account for what I alone have witnessed and experienced while in Idaho's prisons, but it seems everyone is high on something or another.

I for one have refrained from self-medicating (drug use) behind the wall. My past drug use before coming to prison was short-lived, and I have not touched alcohol for twenty-six years. Nevertheless, I am not a prude; I am open-minded to self-medication and am in favor of legalizing recreational marijuana. However, I am saying drug use behind the walls is out of control! Idaho's prisons are overrun with illegal substances. I have seen or heard of heroin, meth, ecstasy (MDMA), GHB, cocaine, steroids, marijuana, and several types of prescription medication, and the newer designer drugs such as bath salts flow as water behind the walls. Bath salts (saltine), no matter what it is being called, are killing the brains of our youth. Too many young Idaho inmates are warping their brains beyond repair with these substances.

I believe the future of Idaho is at risk if we do not respond to this crisis—now. It is suicide; Idaho is perishing by its own hands. I believe Idaho's leadership is well aware of this crisis but fails to respond. By allowing this to continue, they (Idaho's leadership) are able to point to the prison addicts and spew propaganda, frightening the public to strengthen their case of harsher punishments and further incarceration. I truly believe they will do whatever they can to protect their way of life and their pocketbooks and the prison empire that Idaho has built, even if this means destroying the poorer citizens of Idaho.

I have never seen a needle beyond the confinements of a doctor's office or on television until I was sentenced to prison. I have come to learn that four out of five drug users in Idaho prisons are or were intravenous drug users. Hepatitis, HIV and other bloodborne pathogens are common among America's prison population. It was once said to me by an individual, if you didn't have a drug problem going into prison, more than likely you will before you get out. This same individual also said the day he gets out of prison he was going straight into a drug rehab facility for his addiction acquired while in prison. Unfortunately, though I was given the same response by many, many others stated to me that they will continue their drug use once released from prison.

Most nonviolent charges across America are drug charges. Idaho was infamous for jailing and imprisoning even small-time marijuana offenders (though marijuana is still illegal in any form in Idaho, Idaho has loosened their marijuana restrictions somewhat with most offenders possessing small amounts receiving misdemeanor charges). Most of Idaho's surrounding states are marijuana friendly, two with legalized recreational use of marijuana. Individuals coming from these states are targeted and often get busted crossing state lines with small amounts of marijuana. They are frequently sent to a jail (prison for larger amounts), costing the Idaho taxpayer hundreds of thousands of dollars to house and feed these marijuana offenders. Of course it is lawmakers' and law enforcement's intent to generate revenue through fines and confiscations of vehicles and other private property, but most marijuana offenders have small amounts and return home to their home state without paying a dime in fines, thus leaving the Idaho taxpayer flipping the bill. This is bad business for the Idaho taxpayers. Help stop this waste of tax dollars by addressing this situation with a congressman in your area. Please become proactive in your community and question why your tax dollars are being wasted. Idaho deserve better.

I am both amazed and appalled by the many ways contraband gets through the gates of hell. Though inmates are always coming up with new and brazen ways to smuggle drugs and other contraband items into a facility, much comes the old-fashioned way, packed in an inmate's rectum (a.k.a. the prison wallet). During my prison time, I have learned of many ways contraband enters into the prison system here in Idaho. A lot of the drugs, tobacco, and other contraband enter the lower-level facilities (minimum-custody facilities) by the way of *drops* made by friends and families of inmates working community jobs (road crews, fire crews, etc.). Inmates have little to lose if caught with no good time to take away (Idaho does not offer or give good time to its inmates) and there are huge amounts of money to be made from such contraband. A hand-rolled cigarette goes for two dollars, a Chapstick cap full of marijuana for more than twenty-five dollars (the cost is even higher in the medium-security facilities). Most of the contraband entering the lower-level institutions is distributed and stays in the lower-level facilities.

New technology has also added to the contraband problem. In recent times I have heard of drones being used. I am told with this new technology, an inmate can call out for a delivery and have whatever it is within a few hours. I understand why prison officials have not come to terms with this new high tech, technology, I have a hard time grasping the ramifications myself, but I also understand how this technology could become the main line of Idaho's prison contraband problem in the future.

However, most shocking of all is that the majority of all contraband entering into a prison facility is walked right through the prison front door. Some by way of visiting some by way of mail, but most comes by way of corrupt or compromised prison staff. With that being said in 2018 four Idaho Department of Corrections employees (Correctional Officers) were indicted by the FBI. They were all charged with at least one count of conspiracy to aid and abet the distribution of controlled substances, in addition to other charges as well. Unfortunately these individuals are just the tip of the corruption iceberg that plagues IDOC. Corruption runs deep in Idaho, and those who know the truth refer to the Idaho Department of Corrections as being The Idaho Department of Corruption. Remember the psychotic, psychopathic killer who tried to kill me with a prison shank? I once witnessed him pull a cell phone, a large and tightly wrapped bag of chewing tobacco, one Bic lighter, and small bag of marijuana from his asshole. I was totally dumbfounded, amazed by how easily it was for him to pack and remove such large amounts of contraband in and from his rectum. Not only was he a psychotic, psychopathic killer, he was also a psychotic, psychopathic prison drug dealer. And to worsen the situation, for months like clockwork, an ICC staff member would come to our cell asking—rather forcing—me to leave. This prison guard was bringing in drugs for this psychotic, psychopathic killer whom I was forced to live with. Since then, having time to comprehend my blessings, I truly feel lucky to be alive. I realize now what a dangerous situation I was really in. I could have been killed in my sleep, and such a crime could have been easily covered up by dirty prison staff, swept completely under the rug so as not to expose their illegal actions. Never to awake, my throat cut, something this psychotic psychopath had done before in this life. I know now how close to death I was. Though no one can see them, these scars are deep.

Obviously illegal drugs are considered contraband in a prison. However, as I stated earlier, illegal drugs are not the only drug problem within prison walls. The answer to any medical problems by the prison's medical provider is medication. Idaho is notoriously over-medicating their prison population at one of, if not the highest rates in the nation. The majority of inmates agree to the medication for the escape it provides; others agree for the money they can make by selling their medication to others. These medications usually create a more lethargic inmate population that is often easier to control, but this is a very dangerous practice for the inmate themselves. Far too many individuals are walking around like zombies, wacked out of their minds from overmedication, all supplied by the prison. The sad thing is there are many others who need medication and are forced to go without. This is the true insanity of our dysfunctional system.

Another way this madness is allowed to continue is by Idaho's total lack of monitoring, not just the inmates themselves but inmate placing as well as inmates' prison banking accounts. In 2016, there was an inmate suffering from severe short-term memory loss. This individual attributed his mental handicap to have been hit in the head with a hammer. I cannot say with any certainty if there is any truth to his statement or not; however, I can testify to the fact that he had no short-term memory at all. He would get lost after taking a shower or leaving the dayroom, wandering around the tier looking for his cell when all others were locking up for count, making officers well aware of his disability. This man also had a great deal of income but could not remember his pin number to order his commissary (inmates must order commissary on a computer and must use a pin number to gain access). However, other inmates were quick to help. His disability enabled other inmates to take advantage of him, extorting him to pay for their drug use, ordering large amounts of commissary for themselves, forcing him to turn it over after picking it up. Prison officials never picked up on this, allowing it to continue for months. This man bought four pair of shoes in one month, and though inmates are only allowed one pair of personal shoes, this never raised any concern with prison staff.

Let's just say you are lucky enough to get out of prison and then you are forced to go to a halfway house as I and many others like me are forced to do. Faith based halfway and sobriety houses began springing up everywhere under President George W. Bush's term. I am sure President Bush's own battle with alcohol had a lot to do with this, and I am also sure he meant well, but something went awry. The tax cuts and government funding President Bush set aside for these institutions became a source of greed for a majority of these facilities, and this corruption continues today. Again, within the first few hours of being out of prison, I was exposed to drug use at one of these halfway houses.

I have been to a couple different halfway houses in the Boise area, and all were filled with drugs and drug users. In no way did I feel safe when forced to live in a house with people I did not know other than may or may not have seen around a prison yard, especially knowing they were high on Scooby snacks (drugs), paranoid, and willing to do anything but stay sober to stay out of prison.

As I came to learn, there is a major drug problem in Idaho's prison system; then again, I have come to learn America has a serious drug problem. This problem is perpetuated by the billions of dollars made by America's pharmaceutical companies. America's need for opiates is so great that the United States consumes approximately three-fourths of the world's supply (75 percent). Oxycodone, Oxycotton, Norco, morphine, Demerol, Fentanyl, and other painkiller prescriptions flow like water form doctor offices at the glee of greedy pharmaceutical companies. These drugs, more often than not, lead to dependence, and many turn to heroin and other illegal and black-market opiates. Idaho once had, and still has, a huge problem with methamphetamine (of which some or most of the ingredients come from Mexico), but times are changing, Heroin and its opiate friends are the here and now, just around the corner, hidden out of sight of the citizens of Idaho. Heroin has become an epidemic on the east coast. Law enforcement there as well as here in Idaho now carry adrenaline inhalants to give to overdose victims.

I predict heroin and its partners in crime will wreak more havoc in years to come then meth did in the last thirty years, killing hundreds, maybe thousands. And I also predict Idaho's leadership will talk a good game, promising results but doing little. They have to talk the talk for re-election, but the walk would conflict with Idaho's and its incarceration business, and that wouldn't be good business for the pocketbooks of Idaho's leaderships. Please demand your leadership do something about this growing problem before it's too late. Too many of our young citizens are being turned into addicts in our prison system, and that my friend is a disturbing truth. I'm very fortunate I don't have a drug problem because if I was an addict, I would be screwed because the treatment that I have been through while incarcerated in Idaho is not a treatment at all. I truly feel those with addiction issues need professional help. Addiction is a disease, and it can't be cured by sentencing an addict to prison or by a IDOC drug and alcohol counselor who received a certificate after completing an online crash course. Addiction needs to be treated with the same skills and compassion that any other chronic illness would be treated. You can't cure addiction with incarceration. In my opinion, Idaho and IDOC needs to step up and do better or stop wasting tax dollars or treatment programs that continue to fail. Then again, maybe these treatment programs are doing exactly what they are designed to do create recidivism by failure. No matter how you see or judge it's success or failure, it's all bad business for the Idaho taxpayer and to those who are not getting the help that they obvious need while being incarcerated in an Idaho prison.

CHAPTER 10

Sex in Prison

There is a big difference between my first years in an Idaho prison and what it is today in a Idaho prison. Idaho's inmate population has aged on both side of the spectrum, growing both older and younger at the same time. Due to the length of sentences, many of Idaho's inmate populace is now above the age of fifty. However, a majority of the newly sentenced prison inhabitants are younger than ever before. The bulk of Idaho's newly sentenced are straight out of high school, and with this youth comes change, a new area of thought for the inmate population as well as prison staff, and new difficulties for Idaho and its prison system, dealing with homosexuality.

Though Idaho's governor, Butch Otter, has fought tooth and nail against gay marriage and transgender equality, he has been shut down at every turn by the federal government, and he spent many of Idaho's tax dollars fighting a battle that he had no chance in winning, why? Because he does not approve of gay marriage. How is this not discrimination against same-sex marriages by the governor of Idaho? Since then, Idaho has been forced to come into its own. Idaho had no choice but to come out of the closet and face the fact that homosexuality lives and breathes within Idaho's borders and its prison system. A large number of the Idaho prison population is either gay or transgender. Idaho was forced to supply hormone supplements to transgender inmates and now sells bras on the men commissary list. And with the changing laws and looks of men (male inmates with breasts), homosexuality and sexual acts are on the rise within the walls. Sixty percent of Idaho inmates are involved in some type of homosexuality. Additionally on a sadder note during my research the latest survey shows an estimated 4 percent of federal and state prisoners and 3.2 of jail prisoners, reporting one or more incidents of sexual victimization in the past year—that's a little over eighty thousand inmates being sexual victimized while incarcerated, that's a hell of a lot of people being rape in our jails and prisons. Sadly, and I assure you, if you become a victim of a sexual assault while in an Idaho prison you will be treated the same as the person who raped you. No different unless, of course, you happen to be an officer entrusted with your care, then you, the victim will be treated far worse. You will go to the hole (Solitary confinement) while staff conducts an investigation (a very slow process). There is little or no respect shown for what you just went through by prison staff.

Sex in prison, to this point, has been a taboo subject in our society. No one wants to speak of it, yet everybody wants to know about it. I do not claim it was nonexistent until recent years; it is simply was not out in the open, and sex within Idaho's prisons is now "open for business." There is a saying behind the walls, "You're not gay if you quit a week before you get out." This was, of course, started as a joke but has become the truth for too many of Idaho's youth.

Idaho Department of Corrections has a *zero tolerance* for any form of sexual activity and/or conduct between inmates, or inmates and staff, volunteers, contractors, visitors, and even animals (bestiality— apparently, Idaho has a problem with animals being raped). And yes, I have heard of two cases of bestiality within the walls. One was a young man that had been caught many times having sex with dogs. He used to joke about getting into the dog program (a very well-received program in which inmates train dogs for adoption). When first, hearing this, I found it funny, but after a little thought, it sickened my stomach, especially when thinking of how socially accepted these sexual acts had become within the walls and how they could, and were, affecting me. The other case is even more disrturbing.

A man from northern Idaho once told me his delusional behavior began as an adolescent after discovering a dead wolverine in an animal trap. He said he knew his desire was evil but that he could not help himself, and that was the first time he had sex with an animal. However, in his case, it was not just animals. He was serving a life sentence for rape and hinted to having sex with the dead. You may think this case is a rarity, an oddity that does not happen or take place often, but the truth is that Idaho's prison system is a cesspool overflowing with twisted sex offenders.

Again, I am not saying all in prison for sexual acts are irredeemable. I even believe some have been treated unfairly when sentenced for having consensual sex with a person within a couple of years of their own age. Nevertheless, I do believe that lines have to be drawn, that age limits must be in place. And I also believe that majority of sex offenders have a twisted and delusional sexual desire that has little to do with sex and all to do with power and control. And there is a large population of these twisted sex offenders behind Idaho's walls.

The Idaho prison is full of *cho-mos* (child molesters), *mos* (molesters), and all types of sexual predators that have engaged in some type of abnormal sexual acts. There are rapos (rapist), child molesters, baby rapers, diaper sniffers, dipper lickers, baby touchers, playground avengers, and kiddie nippers, who have in some way inflicted injury on the young and weak, permanently scaring them. It is my honest opinion that any one that has stolen the innocence of a child is suffering from an irreversible disease and should never be released into society. Unfortunately, their behavior, more often than not, continues behind the walls.

Prison rape and sexual activity seriously reduce prison safety. The consequences of prison rape and sexual activity include an increase in victimization of the vulnerable, mentally ill, and youthful inmates (especially for the weak and the small, like me). This also increases in the spread of HIV, hepatitis, tuberculosis, and all sexually transmitted diseases (STDs). Racial tension can be heightened because of interracial sexual assaults. Sexual assaults create severe psychological and physical effects to the victims (as I know all too well). It also increases prison suicides and may incite violence against not just inmates but staff as well.

It is also known to increase the risk of insurrection and riot. It can reduce an inmate's ability to successfully transition to the community and follow a law-abiding life style when released. I've come to know this all too well. It often creates post-traumatic stress disorder (PTSD) which I struggle with it every day of my life. I once believed PTSD to be more of an excuse than actual disease, before being raped myself.

There are many other reasons why sexual behavior is inappropriate in prison. None of it involves moral judgment regarding sexual preferences. In a prison setting, sexual relationships, including those that are consensual, create security issues which can foster violence. For example; some inmates do not approve of open homosexuality (same-sex relationships). This can and has created tension and violence to those who are involved in same-sex relations. Fights can occur when a couple breaks up (you do not need to be in prison for that to be a problem), or over jealousies when ones partner is unfaithful (something that is quite frequent). There are also health and safety concerns for all who are in a prison facility, particularly with the transmission of sexually transmitted diseases. Nevertheless, people will be people; there is sex in prison and always will be. Homosexuality has been going on since the beginning of time, and maybe it is time to wake up and smell the coffee and do what we can to help curve the transmission of sexually transmitted diseases.

I do not condone breaking prison rules, nor do I care what sexual preferences another human being has; the truth is, it's none of my business. But what is my business is being forced to live within an environment in which I have no control, an environment that puts my safety and well-being at risk. I feel it is the prison's responsibility to ensure my safety while I am in their care, and I believe the prison must do whatever is needed to ensure my well-being. In order to do this, there must be reform.

I am unsure of the answer to this confusing dilemma, but I do know that many jails and prisons throughout the world and across the United States have made attempts to curve sexual activity and rape within the walls. Some state prisons, have successfully mitigated violence by segregating weaker prisoners from more violent and sexually aggressive inmates during evening hours. Many states freely hand out condoms, some even segregating gay and transgender inmates. I have heard of some states experimenting with coed prison facilities. And many states allow conjugal visits.

Almost every inmate is permitted visits from family members at different intervals. However, conjugal visits—that is, visits where sexual intercourse between inmates and their spouses may occur—are customary throughout the world, particularly in the Scandinavian countries and South America. In Canada, most prisoners are permitted private family visits once every two months for periods of up to seventy-two hours. Within the United States, as of 1998 only six states—California, Connecticut, Mississippi, New Mexico, New York, and Washington—allowed inmates conjugal visits with their spouses. In these jurisdictions, prison administrators consider conjugal visits a special privilege earned through good conduct. Nevertheless, in most US states, prison officials are reluctant to permit conjugal visits because these visits may permit exchanges of contraband and illegal drugs. Officials must weigh the security risks of conjugal visits against the benefit of allowing prisoners to engage in heterosexual activity. Many believe that the lack of heterosexual activity in prisons contributes to increased homosexual activity among inmates. Idaho has so far ignored this growing problem and has not implemented any of these programs.

I feel by acknowledging this problem and being proactive, Idaho could create better living conditions for all as well as reduce sexually transmitted diseases as other states and countries have done. There is no need for Idaho to turn their head and thumb their nose at their gay and transgender population as if ignoring it will deplete it. A safe environment should be provided to people like me while in a prison (heterosexuals). Providing condoms alone would greatly reduce sexually transmitted diseases, saving huge sums of tax dollars in law suits and medical expenses.

Idaho has a large sex offender population. There is little segregation, except for extreme cases, and when walking ISCI's yard, one would think Idaho's sex offenders are protected; of course, in a way they are (there is more segregation at ISCC, but somewhat less in Idaho's other prison institutions). An argument can end up in a hate charge being filed. Show physical aggression, and you will most assuredly be charged.

I have been forced to live with more than one sex offender during my confinement. The worse of which was a sexual predator always on the hunt for young boys (younger inmates). This predator had a fetish with douching (enemas). He had a makeshift bottle that he would fill with a special liquid, and then put this bottle as far up his rectum as he could before releasing the liquid concoction. He seemed to take great pleasure in doing this every night in front of me, two feet away. I could not take it any longer. I rolled myself out of that cell, and when staff questioned me, I just told the truth (something taboo within a prison setting). The messed-up thing was that staff was already aware of his behaviors. I also know of another inmate who is famously known for sticking apples up his rectum. Of course, Ol' Apple Bottom, as the inmates call him, would have to make frequent trips to medical and have the apples professionally removed from his asshole.

At times, prison is like being in a circus sideshow; freaks are everywhere. While living on tier four of main dorm in Idaho's SICI (also known as the farm), I witnessed a young man go to a visit each week with his girlfriend. He would slide his hand up her dress before the visit would end and immediately go back to the tier. There, he would find another inmate waiting for him, and this freak would pay to smell this man's fingers. Once this twisted individual got what he needed, he would immediately get in to the shower to masturbate. Obviously they were both freaks!

Many individuals in Idaho prisons make homemade sex toys out of rubber gloves. They fill these makeshift devices with warm water and lotions and masturbate with them. Inmates often have secretive signs they will put in a cell window alerting their Bunkie (assigned roommate within a cell) to their activity. In a dorm setting it is usually done in the shower, but some (the most deranged) will display such activity right in their bunks, even stare at other men as they do it. Theses freaks are very protective over their masturbation tools and refer to them as their girl, in many cases even given them names. One of my ex-cellmates named his Fee-Fee.

Porn is always in demand; it is highly valued and is as good as cash, better than gold. Inmates have been known to kill for it. No joke—while I was in fourteen house on the yard, a lifer (an inmate who is doing life without parole) stabbed a rider (a short-time pro-grammer) in the face for stealing his porn.

On the less crazy side, for the more normal, they have their shower girls. These are usually laminated soft-porn pictures that can be placed on a shower wall (sometimes more graphic pictures make it in). This is how normal inmates take care of their business, privately masturbating as a fourteen-year-old kid. And yes, I have done this (why do you think I contribute this to be normal). However, we the normal do it privately. And if any one says they have not done this, trust me, they are either lying or have had their prostate removed.

Homosexuals, the gay, and the transgender are actually running the show in Idaho's prison system. Besides the prison's protections, allotments, and accommodations made to medicate the transgender population with female hormone treatment plans, they also have their own gang, the Gay Boy Gangsters (GBG). They are the queens of the ball, the true shot callers in Idaho prisons. And they do not tolerate being called or referred to as a *him* or any other references to the male gender. If by accident you did, you could get a few teeth knocked out for such a mistake (for real). The GBGs are the most popular inmates in Idaho's prison system. Some, maybe even a majority, are more attractive than the female officers working within the prisons; many have larger breasts (no joke). The GBGs are here to stay and are the most protected inmates, you mess with one you and you may end up dealing with half the prison population, not to mention all of the prison staff. The most dangerous inmate in an Idaho prison is a sister (one of the Queens or a GBG), because they can give sexual favors to take anyone out.

These days, everything is out in the open; individuals are always hugging and kissing one another. Holding hands has become a normal occurrence. I realize times are changing and all deserve equality and respect, but Idaho's prison system is out of control. Prison staff have tried to ignore this growing problem by hiding their heads in the sand.

There is a saying many inmates refer to: "What happens in prison stays in prison." It was a saying that was started to detour inmates from telling on one another but has become something else. Many men do not want their families to know of their homosexual activities and are willing to do anything to keep it hidden from a wife or parent.

No one wants to take a sexually transmitted disease home to their wife or girlfriend. No one wants to risk giving their children or loved ones AIDS, but it happens. Some say it is only gay if you continue in homosexual acts after leaving prison—not true. A lot of young kids come in straight and leave prison gay. I have personally witnessed this fact. This creates problems with not just Idaho's youth but with many across America. Many men become confused, people get hurt, and families are being destroyed. I truly believe Idaho is its own worst enemy with no regards to its citizens or their future.

If you are a resident in the state of Idaho, there is a greater chance that you are living with a register sex offender in your neighborhood. And to make a bad situation worse, hundreds—possibly thousands—of unregistered sex offenders are currently being released from an Idaho prison. They are the ones that were sentenced for drug possession or drunk driving and have then learned this twisted sexual behavior behind the walls of a Idaho prison.

CHAPTER 11

Future Criminals for Life

I am sure the average American is unaware that a prison sentence is about survival: it is sink or swim, adapt or die. Most people are clueless of what individuals have to live with and endure in attempts to survive behind the walls. I have shared examples of what I have been forced to live through. I have tried to explain the daily fear and torment I was forced to withstand and endure, the humility of being raped while neatly tucked away behind the walls.

I was a grown man when first sentenced to prison. I turned forty my first birthday behind the walls. My children were also grown, and I had no child support to pay or had anyone depending on me for financial support. I was a productive human being, a man who had worked all my life, who paid taxes. I lived what I believed to be a normal life. I conformed and behaved with society's moral values, devolved proper social skills throughout my life. I knew who I was, taking pride in being a good, kind, and caring person who always showed respect toward others.

I was very fortunate; I had good, loving, and hardworking parents (both of them). My parents provided a clean, safe home for me and my siblings, one that was totally drug- and alcohol-free. My parents taught me good moral values and a lot about life itself. Without their guidance, I would have never become the man that I am today, the kind, caring, respectful man who lives life to the fullest each and every day. I thank both the Lord and them for who I am.

My years in prison have opened my eyes; I have come to know the disgusting truth about life on the other side of the tracks. I'm not from Idaho never lived here before going to prison. Now that I have spent some time here (more importantly, in prison here), I have seen the true madness of incarceration as a business, how it is affecting the young and poor citizens of Idaho. It is the youth of Idaho who are paying the price of this abusive madness, and with every day, this abusive madness is allowed to continue; more and more lives are being destroyed by Idaho's greedy politicians. An outsider looking in, such as President Obama, would call this true insanity. Idaho is destroying its young, therefore destroying itself by its own hands. Why does Idaho continue to shoot itself in the foot pausing only long enough to reload, when will this madness end?

America's greatest resource dwells within the well-being of our children. Our children are the future. They are the future taxpayers, the ones that will pay for our roads, libraries, and Social Security. Idaho is destroying this precious resource and its own future by undereducating that very resource. Of all states, Idaho is near the bottom, in education. Idaho's prison budget rivals its education budget dollar for dollar. I am both alarmed and dumfounded by this, and every Idaho resident should be too. This, in no way, should be accepted or tolerated. Why has Idaho given up on the future? Why are Idaho's public servants it's leadership failing Idaho in such a way? Why are they destroying not just your future but the future of our nation? This madness must stop.

The common theme through my years of incarceration has been the never-ending supply of under educated young adults walking through the gates of hell neatly tucked away and hidden from public scrutiny. These are not unintelligent young men or women and, in fact, in most cases it is just the opposite. Intelligence is not measured by knowing a lot of things but how one uses the things they know. Many of the newly convicted youth have simply not needed or have found no use for conventional knowledge. The type of knowledge they have found useful is known as *street smarts,* meaning they have learned to live in and by less desirable means than the greater part of society. A large number are also immature or have suffered some type of abuse or mistreatment. Many have learning disabilities that have been ignored or went undiagnosed for years. Many have been in and out of juvenile detention centers and foster homes, with a large percentage of those having been abused by caretakers or an unfair justice system, which in turn creates under educated and resentful adults. And because of these earlier abuses inflicted, an even smaller amount enters an institution with respect for authority or the law.

Besides lacking in the social skills that are created in a caring environment or family setting, most have not learned or have been taught self-control or communication skills, and many refuse to accept or know how to respond to criticism. Few are able to control emotions, feelings, or manage anger, stress, and anxiety. Most are angry and unformed, unshaped vessels when entering the gates of hell and are susceptible to peer pressure. And most frightening is what happens to them behind the walls, what they learn before being released.

Very few of the young entering prison have any job skills; some have never held a job at all (other than selling of drugs). A large number has yet to obtain a driver's license and even fewer have had a checking account, much less the ability or knowledge of how to balance one. I have meet many that could not read or write. The majority has a very small vocabulary, and the use of profanity is widespread. Many come from broken homes where a parent or parents are drug and alcohol users (abusers). Many have parents that have been convicted of small drug offenses and have been sentenced to prison themselves, perpetuating the incarceration problem. A family tradition in Idaho has become doing time in prison with a parent.

During my incarceration, I have come to know and have met many fathers and sons that were doing time in prison together. This tradition is growing—expanding to far too many families, destroying our youth and our future. Think about a kid growing up with a parent in prison (a sad situation, right?). Now think about this becoming a normal situation not just for them but for their friends and peers. One in twenty-five adult males in Idaho is in prison or on parole. This means every family in Idaho knows someone in prison or has a family member in prison themselves. Though this is in no way normal, it has become the norm. This perpetuation of incarceration has to end.

Prison is not the future for America's youth. America's future lies in educating our children. Idaho, especially, has built an empire based on its justice system. Idaho has and will protect this empire at all cost their actions prove this with each small time felony conviction and overly excessive prison sentences. Education and the well-being of the young (the future of Idaho) has taken a back seat and become second at best to this empire of the injustice that Idaho has created, created off the blood and tears of its very citizens. Idaho without question is out of control and the children of Idaho are paying a high price for its greed!

As I was attempting to comprehend this perpetuating madness, pressing myself to scribe the words you now read, I was suddenly sickened with each touch of key, each word spelled out. My thinking was these children have parents, and these parents must be held accountable. They have a part in this as well; they are ones failing their children, not doing their job as a parent. But I have come to realize that the parents of this new generation of Idaho's inmates have been victims of Idaho's unjust justice system and corrupt politicians themselves. And now, even as I write this, I feel even more confused, appalled, and sickened.

I was blessed to have both of my parents. My parents were and still are law-abiding, tax-paying citizens, yet I have still ended up in prison. This alone tells me it must be more, that the parents cannot be completely to blame. The sad truth is that there are a lot of kids not awarded an opportunity in life because America, and states like Idaho is abusing its authority for profit. The majority of all inmates in an Idaho prison have been sentenced for what would have been a misdemeanor in other states. Huge numbers of Idaho's youth are growing up without a parent because the state has incarcerated their mothers and fathers for excessive amounts of time behind bars for little more than a misdemeanor in other states. When does this perpetuating madness end?

My hope is that after reading my words, we unite, stand together, and become proactive. Not just in Idaho but all of America must become proactive and insist our lawmakers begin prison reform, doing away with excessive mandatory sentencing, especially for small-time drug charges. American addicts are the victims. They may have sold small amounts to supply their habits, but that is the nature of the beast. They are not the ones bringing the drugs across our borders and distributing them in our neighborhoods. They are not the ones handing out opium narcotic prescriptions as if they were candy. No, they are the victims of not just corrupt South American drug lords or other countries officials but also the victims of our own politicians and our counties refusal to stop this problem at its source. You have to ask yourself, why have our politicians turned their backs on this problem?

A top aid in the Nixon administration openly admitted that Nixon's War on Drugs was a way to curve and prevent the poor (who usually vote democrat), particularly African-Americans and the so-called *hippies* from voting. Once convicted of a felony, politicians stripped the rights of those convicted (voting rights and the right to bear arms among others). In other words, the Nixon administration imprisoned what they considered the undesirables to advance their parties (the Republican Party) agenda. In doing so, our politicians also figured out they could better control the rest of the population through scare tactics. Both Nixon and Regan declared drugs to be the greatest threat our nation has ever seen, although our last three presidents openly admitted to smoking marijuana. And though our last three presidents said this, marijuana remains prohibited federally and is number one in all arrest in the United States (more people are arrested for marijuana charges than any other crime)

After discovering they could control populations and advance their agenda through incarceration and scare tactics, our politicians also discovered there was money to be made by incarceration. Remember that George W. Bush's vice president, Dick Chaney, owns one of the largest prisons for profit businesses in the United States, the GEO Corporation, and business was very good while he was in power. This is not in any way helping our country and should not be tolerated. For a lawmaker to own such a business and push for increased laws and incarceration is in direct conflict with the very office they hold.

There was a time when the young convicted of crimes were given an option of joining the military or go to prison (both the Korean and the Vietnamese era, and I certainly don't believe a felony would prevent anyone from enlisting in the war effort during World War II). This program worked; it benefitted America as well as huge numbers of Americans themselves. After serving our country, these young men went on to lead productive lives, they were better suited to gain employment and contribute to our economy. They paid taxes, started families, and bought homes and cars. Yet this program and programs like it have fallen to the wayside. Why, why are we not building up our youth empowering them with tools for success? Instead our American justice system exploits them and then tears them down, leaving them broken. For worst than they were before being incarcerated.

What do you think happens to a kid when an unjust system puts them in prison without any self-empowerment such as education or vocational training? Do we really feel safer? Do any of us believe that somehow a miracle happens and are magically cured just because they went to prison, think again. What do you think a kid learns once the state like Idaho sends them to prison? Kids with little or no education or social skills and no job skills—what do you think happens to them once they are released?

Idaho, overall, has an 85 percent recidivism rate. This means 85 of every 100 inmates return to prison, sadly the majority of them return back to prison within the same year of release. This high rate of recidivism is evidence that Idaho's current prison business is and has been failing to do its job, and wasting tax dollars. I believe its time we hold those accountable for not doing the job Idaho tax payers are paying them to do. Regardless, the greatest numbers of those inmates that somehow make it and do not come back are over the age of fifty. This means the prospects for the convicted young in Idaho is very bleak. Once a young man walks through the gates, Idaho has lain out their future. States like Idaho are stealing our youth, turning our children into monsters who become criminals for life, and that is a true crime against humanity.

By Idaho's own statistics, a young person has little chance of getting out and staying out of prison until they turn fifty, a large number then going on to Disability Social Security, never contributing to our economy, paying taxes, or learning any life skills. They have been to prison and received a PhD in how to be a criminal for life. The chances of them returning to prison are virtually guaranteed, so what are we giving these young men to look forward to? Idaho and the prison system provide no education, no help, and no hope, nothing to help a person become successful after leaving prison. With nothing to look forward to, no job skills or education, what makes anyone believe these young men would change their criminal behavior? This insane madness must be stopped. Idaho and its public servants must be held accountable for failing Idaho. Education and job training must be a priority, not just in Idaho but all of America. Education and job training are the keys to prison reform, the key to America's success.

There was once a program where businesses were allowed tax breaks for hiring newly released felons. Vocational rehabilitation (Volc-rehab) was also good to help with tools and work clothing. However, Volc-rehab funding has been drastically cut and the tax cut program completely eliminated.

I am going to pretend for a moment that I am a businessman looking to expand my business and the state of Idaho is an option. As I did my due diligence and investigated Idaho, I have come to learn Idaho has one the lowest amount of high school graduates and one of the largest populations of individuals who are on parole or probation, and an above average drug problem in the United States. Although the tax incentive and Volc-rehab programs may have given me cause to give ex-cons a chance. However, without such programs and knowing that a huge population of Idaho's labor market "work force" are either on probation or parole, felons, under educated, may or may not be under the influence. So, why would I or any other corporation have any incentive (other than Idaho's unlivable wages) to do business in Idaho? Idaho is truly destroying its future for generations to come.

I have witnessed firsthand how Idaho is creating monsters who become criminals for life. Though they may show remorse and/or regrets, our convicted youth are constantly told they are worthless and have no future. For myself, I was not so easily impressed, swayed, or tempted by gangs and the other evil ways of prison life. But I came in at nearly forty years old and knowing who I was. Sure, I have had my bouts with depression and evil thoughts of suicide after the beatings and the rape I endured. Though I still struggle with PTSD and depression, I feel truly lucky to have survived and not have taken my own life. Nevertheless, the sad truth is that a large majority of young inmates succumb to the evil ways of prison mentality, and many that endured what I have gone through escape it by the use of drugs or, worst, suicide.

The only growth promoted behind the walls is how to abuse, lie, cheat, steal, con, or manipulate for immediate gratification. Thus, leading to the escape of reality by drug use (often promoted by the prison itself). These kids are destroying their still-developing brains with the toxic waste they have been putting into their bodies, toxic waste often prescribed by the prison itself in an attempt to create a more lethargic population. This is in no way good for them or Idaho, for one day these state-created monsters will be released and may move next door to you. These are not the scum of the earth but impressionable kids that have been disregarded, thrown away while politicians line their pockets by selling lucrative state contracts and try to convince the rest of their state's population it was for the good of society.

Our young and impressionable may need a firm hand once in a while, but they also need love and guidance. They need love the most when they seem to deserve it the least. How do we as a society expect someone never shown compassion to show it themselves? Prison is not always the answer to mistakes made; there are alternative solutions. By giving up on the children of today, we are therefore giving up on tomorrow. We as a society must do better. We must stop putting money ahead of lives. There is an old saying: "You are either part of the solution or part of the problem." Please become part of the solution. Our children's future is in desperate need of help. Incarceration is taking everything from them and not given anything back to reform or rehabilitate. This madness has to end. This madness cannot be tolerated or accepted any longer!

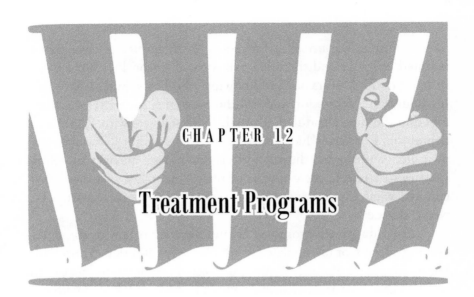

CHAPTER 12

Treatment Programs

I experienced my first treatment program after being arrested and entering the Ada county jail. During the ongoing court proceedings, my public defender suggested that I attend a treatment program before sentencing. I took his advice and immediately signed up for the available programs offered at the Ada county jail.

I found myself enrolled in a cognitive based program called Moral Recognition Therapy (MRT) and a drug and chemical dependency program that I know only as ABC. Though taking the ABC program, I am still unaware what the letters stand for. These two treatment programs were offered at one hundred dollars each, which was to be paid in advance. I was fortunate enough to have the money and eagerly paid the two hundred dollars required for these two cognitive-based classes. I entered into these programs with a good attitude, wanting to take as much away from them as possible. However, my excitement quickly changed once I realized these treatment programs had little value. Both of these programs were to span a three-month period, but in the Ada county jail, these programs are manipulated by staff into a crash course done in eight one hour sessions in a months' time.

During my second stay at the Ada county jail, my public defender again suggested that I take part in treatment program before sentencing. My public defender stated that I would more likely than not be sentenced to mandated treatment program and that it would look good if I took the initiative and attended the treatment programs before being forced to. Though less eager than the first time, I signed up, but this time, the programs had doubled in price, two hundred dollars each. Again, I was fortunate enough to be able to pay the out-of-pocket expense, four hundred dollars for the two crash courses that had no value whatsoever during my sentencing or in general. They were worthless and useless, and I, as well as many others, left these classes feeling ripped off by these phony treatment programs. I feel this was fraud by deception, committed by my public defender, the courts, and by the Ada county jail and its staff. To my knowledge, this fraud is still going on today.

During my third arrest and detainment in the Ada county jail, when my public defender suggested I take part in a treatment program. I agreed but insisted on funding to pay for it. I filled out the proper paperwork and turned it in. However, I was denied. To make a long story short, I did not take part in any treatment program at that time because I did not qualify for the funding. It seems Idaho is only big on treatment programs if there is money involved, money to be made by the counties and county officials. Think about it—does it really make sense to force someone to take the same cognitive program three times if there was not money involved?

I have witnessed and learned that if sentenced to take part in treatment programs at the jail and have no money to pay for it, individuals may wait months in the Ada county jail at the expense of taxpayers. This is state-ordered kidnapping for ransom. This system is designed to hold Idaho's citizen's hostage until the state-ordered ransom money is paid. This is outright corruption by Idaho and its public servants. These county programs that have little or no value are being forced down the throats of those unfortunate enough to be sentenced to them, usually at the expense of taxpayers. This out of control system only works through intimidation and scare tactics, intimidating inmates and scaring the public into flipping the bill. How is this right or legal?

While detained in Elmore County, inmates (detainees) had a choice, an option. Many were involved in treatment and programing such as Narcotics Anonymous (NA) and Alcoholics Anonymous (AA). Meetings were held every week by outside volunteers, at no expense to inmates or tax payers. Inmates did not feel intimidated and began attending these meetings hoping to make real changes in their lives. Many of the volunteers were former inmates and knew how to relate to those incarcerated. All the volunteers were alcoholics or drug addicts. All attending these meeting could see the value in these programs, all could feel the weight in the volunteers' words, and all attending wanted what the volunteer speakers had, wanting the changes the volunteers had made in their lives.

I have spent a lot a time in the Ada County jail and have never known anyone that was given the opportunity to better themselves by attending self-help meeting such as Narcotics Anonymous (NA) and/or Alcoholics Anonymous (AA). Drug use also ran rampant in Ada County, with attitudes of the inmate population seeming unwilling to change. Whereas Elmore County had no drug use inside the walls that I knew of, and inmate population seemed eager to change. I contribute this to the volunteer AA and NA programs the jail allowed in.

In the Idaho prison system, inmates must participate in treatment programs before being released. Programming pathways (treatment to be taken) are assigned by case managers during the intake process. During my incarceration, I have participated in every treatment program that the Idaho Department of Corrections had to offer (with the exception of sex offender programs).

My prison program resumé consists of Moral Recognition Therapy (MRT), which I took twice. MRT was three months long, (I spent a total of six months in MRT). I have taken Anger Management three times, each time taking three months to complete (a total of nine months). I also participated in a pre-release class twice, (a total of four months). I also had the pleasure in participating in Idaho's Therapeutic Community Program (TC Program), a nine-month program. The TC program includes programs such as Cognitive Self-Change (CSC), Tap-19, Matrix, and Relapse Prevention (RP). I was in this program fourteen months. I also participated in the Residential Drug Alcohol Program (R-DAP) that was six months long. I did a total of three years and three months of treatment programs while in the Idaho Department of Corrections. But as of recent times, all the programs I have just mentioned have been discontinued, no longer being facilitated at any of Idaho's correctional facilities.

Why is that? you ask. Well, let me try to break it down. The truth is all these treatment programs are successful everywhere but Idaho. They failed because the Idaho Department of Corrections allowed them to fail, allowing the facilitators who ran and operated the treatment programs to do whatever they chose. The treatment programs wandered so off track that they lost their true meaning. The facilitators themselves were behaving like dictators, robbing the opportunity of inmate's success, and this failure cost Idaho taxpayers billions of dollars.

I had one facilitator who grew up in a red community, not a Republican but a Communist community. Her father is a card-carrying communist here in America with a long FBI file. I believed her views to be distorted and one-sided, not exactly helpful in a treatment program. Many of the facilitators were fired or released from their jobs. The program director was fired for sexual harassment in 2012. The counselor he had harassed was later fired for drug use and mingling with inmates that had been released. The counselors that seemingly enjoyed the sexual role-playing that inmates were forced to participate in were admitted lesbians or homosexuals. One female counselor bragged of being passed around like a joint (a marijuana cigarette) for sexual favors at the Sturgis, South Dakota, biker rally. I also saw pictures of a drug and alcohol counselor, drunk and celebrating the 2013 Super Bowl game in a Boise sports bar.

What I was forced to endure while participating in the TC program was more traumatizing then helpful. Though I tried to do my best, I constantly felt as if I were in a living nightmare. I was in a constant state of confusion, put down and verbally abused by staff as well as other inmates. I went backward; I felt lost while trying to understand what was going on. There was no uniformity between facilitators, each contradicting the other, confusing every group. As the groups attempted to step forward, it seemed the counselors or the rules would change confusing me and the group, forcing all to take two steps back.

Inmates involved in the TC program are forced to participate in role plays with sexual overtones, such as licking an invisible ice-cream cone or popsicle, eating a burrito that is too hot to handle, or acting as a valley girl breaking up with her boyfriend. During Christmas, I was forced to sing Christmas songs that I had never heard before, by myself for the entertainment of staff. Inmates are also forced to hold others accountable through a ticket process that is much like acting like a prison snitch. I had learned early on that telling on another inmate never turns out good, and in fact, I had been beaten for simply being suspected of telling on others behind the walls. I refused to participate in this activity and was removed from the program twice before conforming. I was later beaten for my so-called telling on others while inside the program.

This torturous program stole my self-worth, my mental health, even my physical well-being. By the time I left the TC program, I was a train wreck; I was lost, confused, and broken. Even after returning home, I did not know how to respond to others. I trusted no one, isolating myself to the point that I could not enter a crowded building or grocery store. I wanted desperately to be with and around my family members, but once with them, I became paranoid and could not wait to get away.

This TC program failed me and others like me because IDOC allowed it to fail. There was no outside or impartial oversight. There were no checks and balances to ensure programs were run correctly. And even more importantly, there was no oversight to ensure these programs were working. All recidivism information leads to the same conclusion: there is virtually no difference in recidivism rates between inmates completing the TC program and those who have not (though at the time Idaho claimed there was). These programs were forced upon inmates (do the TC or stay in prison), then ruined the lives of those who went through them. In turn, ruining the lives of inmates' loved ones and children by doing just the opposite of what they were intended. The TC program did not help inmates recognize problems within themselves but created even greater ones.

I realize many of you may think what I am saying to be completely ludicrous or possibly even a total fabrication, but of August 1, 2016, the Idaho's Department of Corrections has gutted and replaced all of their programs. Director of prisons, Kevin Kemp, even mentioned the sexual role plays and the rate or recidivism to be the main contributing factors in this radical replacement (though I have firsthand knowledge that inmate lawsuits have also played a huge roll in this decision). Idaho inmates are now participating in a University of Cincinnati model treatment program.

I for one have participated in all the Cincinnati model programs (with the exception of the sexual programs), starting with Thinking for a Change (TFAC), which is a twenty-week program. I have also participated in the Cognitive Behavioral Interventions—Substance Abuse (CBI-SA), a fifteen-week program, and Aggression Replacement Training (ART), which was a thirty-week program (though the group that I was in completed this program in eight weeks). And on October 19th 2017, I completed IDOC newest treatment program. Cognitive Intervention program known as advance practices. From start to finish there was nineteen class dates, take out three days when there was no class for unknown reasons. All together in total, I went to sixteen advance practices treatment programs classes. And only three of these classes were longer than sixty minutes, all the rest were less than sixty minutes. The group that I was with started with twelve individuals, and by October 19th, there were only seven of us left who completed the program. For the others, I believe they were removed from the program due to their drug use while participating in this program. Additionally, I find it odd that on my certificate that I had received, it said I satisfactory completed 37.5 hours of advance practices training by the University of Cincinnati.

Truth is the group that I was with had less than nineteen hours of class time. After completing these newer programs I have spent four years in IDOC Treatment programs while behind the walls. I am a person who likes to listen and learn, but I must admit, I don't remember a thing about any of the treatment programs I was involved in, I just don't. But I will never forget the fear, the stress the abuse that I experience and witness while participating in IDOC Treatment programs.

The current treatment programs facilitated by the Idaho Department of Corrections (the Cincinnati model) has the potential to be helpful, but so did the past treatment programs. Unfortunately, the Cincinnati programs will fail as well, and it will waste tax dollars in the process. Inmates are being forced to participate in treatment programs before being released from prison. This alone creates an unproductive environment in which inmates will comply but not conform. For the majority, getting out is their only goal, the only reason they are participating in any treatment programs. This drastically drags down the entire program.

Inmates begin faking their way through by trying to gain the approval of the instructor, who in turn devotes a lot of time and effort into teaching a person who is conning them. Inmates who are truly trying to better themselves are often more reclusive, which leads instructors to believe they are not trying as hard as the ones conning them, which frustrates the ones that really want to better themselves. Soon these inmates simply want to get through the program and simply go home as the rest.

Now that I have completed these programs and experienced them, what I have seen and witnessed was not helpful in any way to inmates trying to better themselves. I have also come to learn that inmates at ICC who were recently participating in the Cincinnati based treatment programs were given random drug tests, in which seventy of the seventy-five tested were found to have illegal drugs in their system (this same thing happened in 2012). It is a sad truth that a majority of inmates forced to participate do not care or want help in any way or form, and they take away from those who do want the help.

Another problem is how these newer treatment programs are being facilitated within Idaho Department of Corrections. After eliminating their existing programs, IDOC was beginning to be backed up with inmates waiting to get through the program and be released. Once implementing the Cincinnati programs, IDOC began running inmates through these new treatment programs at alarming rates, as if cattle, sheep, or a cash crop. Even more worrisome, IDOC continues this unproductive behavior and inmates are still being pushed through as if cattle. I witnessed many inmates who could not read or write, who could not do the work, and a lot who could not even speak English. As long as they showed up each class, making an appearance, they passed the class and were released. This is taking away from the true value of the programs, from those who really want and need help. This insanity is creating and producing future criminals who stay drug addicts for life.

Though I have experimented with self-medication, I feel very fortunate not to have a substance abuse problem. However, not experiencing this type of problem has also left a void in my understanding of substance abuse. Throughout my time within prison treatment programs, all facilitators have said relapse is a part of recovery, so of course addicts hearing this think and believe relapse is part of recovery. This seems distorted to me. I cannot help but wonder if addicts interpret this as an excuse for their relapses, but as I said, I was lucky not to have a drug problem, and understanding these powerful demons are a near impossibility for me. I just feel if that is what is going to be taught in the prison treatment programs, then probation and parole officers should consider this when they are violating an addict for failing a drug test. When Idaho's own treatment programs are using this type of language and if everyone knows that relapse is part of recovery, then why are addicts still violated for relapsing? This is truly a form of deception by IDOC that creates recidivism.

With everything I have experienced in the state of Idaho regulated treatment programs, the more I believe they are designed to fail not just me but every taxpayer in the entire state of Idaho. Although I am more than sure our politicians want to protect the prison for profit empire they have created, this failure has to be about more than just protecting their money. There are too many good people involved to be some kind of state-run conspiracy. Though I have focused on the counselors underperforming in most of this chapter, I have to admit that most mean well even if their tactics are misguided, that it is more than just a job for a majority of Idaho's treatment program facilitators. Nevertheless, I also believe the treatment programs are only as good as the ones who are facilitating them. I believe true success rates begin with a willingness to change. We as a society cannot force change by waving some kind of magic wand, no more than a treatment center facilitators.

Because Idaho's treatment programs are crammed down the throats of all, it lessens the entire recovery system. It is human nature to kick against the goad, fight back when those seen as in power continually force their will upon others. Treatment programs are about recovery, helping individuals find self-worth and become successful and productive. Unfortunately, Idaho's treatment programs tear a person down, breaking them, creating more and possibly lifelong problems. Men and women, young fathers and mothers are leaving these treatment facilities with little or no hope.

I believe the answer to be in voluntary participation as with the AA and NA programs of Elmore County. If we really want to see change, then we must stop forcing programs on those who are only willing to comply long enough to get out of prison. I once believed that incentives such as good time would be an appropriate means of filling the prison treatment programs but have since reconsidered. After considering this thought, I have decided it would have the same effect as forcing inmates to enter into treatment; inmates would comply to receive their good time but not conform. However, I do still believe incentives should be in place. Incentives such as better food and living conditions, better visits, and weekend family passes for inmates about to be released. I also believe inmates graduating these programs should be guaranteed six months at a community work release center where they be allowed to attend outside AA and NA meetings and make a proper transition back into the community.

I realize some may believe that there would be too great of risk involved in what I am suggesting. And I admit there are some that may abuse the type of system I am in favor of, but I am also sure the benefits would far outweigh the risk, and the success rates would be unheard of. The inmates I am referring to will be released one day whether they go through any programming or not. They will be your neighbors and coworkers. They may even be the people influencing your children. So I say to those who believe the risk to be too much, are you willing to risk your children and neighborhoods? Are you willing to take the risk of an untreated (or undertreated) addict, whose problems worsened in prison, move in next to you and influence your children?

Becoming proactive in your community today is a start in stopping this madness, this insanity (Einstein described insanity as doing the same things over and over, expecting different results). Question Idaho's leaderships, their motives, question why tax dollars are being wasted on treatment programs that do not work, and question the manipulated success rates of these programs. This is fraud by deception, and it should be illegal, yet is happening every day here in Idaho as well as other states across our nation. We must insist on common sense programing that works if we want real change.

CHAPTER 13

Working for the System

M y experience with the Boise Police Department has been disturb-ing on many levels. At the time of my first arrest, after breaking my mother's truck window in 2009, Boise officers asked me to come out of the house using a loudspeaker. Though surprised because I did not know police had arrived, I fully cooperated and did as requested, only to find thirty guns drawn on me when exiting my residence.

I understand that domestic disputes are one of the most danger-ous situations for police and there is always an increased awareness in such circumstances. However, in this instance, though I did not directly place the call, I was the one that initiated the summons to police by requesting my mother to place the call. After exiting my residence with my hands held in the air as requested, I was immedi-ately smashed face first on the ground and covered by officers plac-ing knees to my spine and neck area as they restrained my hands in cuffs. I was then pulled from the ground by my hair and violently forced into the back of a patrol car, the door slammed on my foot before I could pull it in. This was my very first arrest by the Boise Police Department, my first look into their brutal and indifferent procedures.

The second time I was arrested was by my parole officer. She and her partner were civil and did not hurt me physically. However, they left me confused and wondering what was happening, what was going on. It had an air of a mental game, which I also consider abuse.

My third arrest came after I went to the Boise Police Department to ask for help. While there I was suddenly surrounded by police and roughly manhandled. I was informed they were detaining me as I was pushed into a room and immediately questioned by three different officers at the same time. They purposely confused me by asking different questions in rapid secession. When I asked if I needed a lawyer, I was violently slammed against a wall, handcuffed and arrested for domestic battery. Apparently, Idaho police officers do not have to read or tell you of your rights (Miranda Rights). These charges were later dismissed after a police audio recording revealed the victim's statements (my wife's statements) were not only coerced, but in fact, coached by a Boise police officer on what to write on a victims statement form (in short this officer influence/help a person to lie on a police report). Obviously, this Boise police officer had forgot to turn off his recording device, lucky me, he did not.

Over the years, I have had the privilege of reading many Boise's Police Department's arrest reports. I have found they all share common similarities—all are vague and lacking in actual facts other than times or places, and most are often sloppy and poorly written (it seems Idaho's illiterate are not simply restricted to its prison population). Nevertheless, the most frightening similarities are that all seemed to be based on the opinions and beliefs of the arresting officers. I was truly surprised by this discovery. I had, to this point in my life, believed police were fair, that their objectives were to be honest, just, and as accurate as possible. Needless to say, my views have drastically changed.

Though the Boise area has one of the lowest crime rates in the nation, I have come to learn that the Boise Police Department has one of the highest rates of deadly force (police shootings). As I was writing this chapter, the Boise area had reported three different police shootings in a twenty-four-hour period. However, deadly force is not restricted to the Boise area.

There seems to be an influx of police shootings of unarmed citizens all across the United States, creating outrage in our cities and towns, especially in the African-American communities where a large majority of these deadly shootings are taking place. Two of the most famous incidents caught on tape were the Rodney King beating that took place in Los Angeles, California, and more recently, the shooting of an unarmed black man, Michael Brown, in Ferguson, Missouri, starting the Black Lives Matter movement. But since then, many others have taken place.

An unarmed black man was recently shot and killed by a female officer while in the middle of a roadway holding his hands above his head. Another black man was shot at a Texas gas station while reaching for his wallet at an officer's request. And more recently, charges were filed on another officer for shooting and killing a middle school janitor in Minnesota, a well-liked black man who was said to be a role model for many students. He was shot in the passenger seat as he reached for his wallet at the request of the officer.

A black woman was stopped for failure to use a turning signal and was verbally abused for smoking a cigarette. She was forced from her car, arrested, and taken to jail where she was later found dead in her cell. Another black man, Eric Gardner, was choked to death on the streets of New York for selling loose cigarettes. This man was pleading with officers, telling them he could not breathe, but the relentless officers were determined to keep this person off the streets, strangling him to death.

Another man of color was stopped for a broken taillight. The man tried to flee, fearing a warrant for back child support and was shot in the back multiple times. On this video recording obtained by a Dominican Republic immigrant, this officer was seen planting evidence. This officer, who has been arrested and is facing murder charges, claims the shooting was justified because he was in fear of his life. In Baltimore, Maryland, police arrested a black man who died of a broken spine during transport to the jail. Who breaks their spine during a car ride in which there is no accident? Charges were filed on the five officers involved, but not a single conviction was obtained.

Apparently, the killing of this unarmed man that was already in custody was justified.

These police executions are not just reserved for the black communities; poor white men also suffer these atrocities. A young white man on his first date stopped at a fast food restaurant. His date was approached by an undercover officer and asked if she wanted to buy a small amount of marijuana. The young man went to his car while his date made the transaction. As this young woman was getting into the car, police rushed in. The young man, who was already backing out, continued to back out before putting the car in gear and starting off. He was shot several times in the back and neck area, dying at the scene. Though the officer had shot this young man in the back as he was driving off, this trained veteran public servant claimed he was in fear for his life and no charges were ever filed. More recently, a white woman was brutally punched in the face by an Arizona officer as horrified bystanders watched and told this abusive officer that there was no need of such force. It was only when bystanders informed the women that they were filming the attack. That's when the police officer calmed himself and turned on his own body camera.

An Idaho rancher was also recently shot and killed by two Idaho deputy sheriff officers. Witnesses reportedly gave varying statements, but officers claimed the man pointed a rifle at them. The shooting was found to be justified because officers were said to be in fear of their lives. This story has never made any sense to me because no way will I ever believe that an Idaho rancher who has legally hunted big game his entire life could, at close range, point a rifle at the police with the intention of harming them without doing exactly that, harming them. I truly believe a man that has handled a rifle his entire life, such as that Idaho rancher, could have shot the officers from his hip, without even aiming if he wanted to. There is no other way to say it. This Idaho rancher was murdered. I do truly know now that I was blessed. I could have easily become a victim of a trigger-happy cop the day of my first arrest.

This type of violence is not a new phenomenon; it is not something that has started over the last few years, but has been going on for a long time. It is simply beginning to surface because of the new technology that allows citizens the capability of capturing these incidents of film. However, though police departments claim transparency, they are reluctant to equip themselves with this new technology themselves and have been known to threaten, arrest, and even abuse those who are willing to record them as they abuse others. Recently, a group of college students were actually thrown to the ground and beaten with police night sticks for recording officers engaging with demonstrators. Nevertheless, others caught this brutal attack as well. What is new is the disturbing trend of officers being injured by gun violence.

Though the numbers of violent crimes across the United States is down, not only are the number of officer involved shootings up, but officers being injured or killed is up as well. The number of officers being killed by gunshot in the line of duty is up nearly 67 percent, from approximately thirty-five in 2015, to sixty in 2016. Many of these shootings are contributed as retaliation of police killings of unarmed citizens, mostly unarmed black men. Some are contributed to terrorism. I also personally contribute the rise in violence against police to an unfair justice system. I do not condone the shooting of officers no more than I approve of officers shootings of citizens. However I also contribute these shooting to a justice system that harshly punishes the poor while the wealthy go unscathed. When people are pushed into a corner, they begin to push back. Even mice will fight when they feel there is no other option.

The violence and abuse does not stop after a suspect is taken into custody. Ask Freddy Gray, the Baltimore man that died of a broken spine during a routine transport, or Sandra Bland, the black woman found dead in her cell after being arrested for failure to use a turn signal and smoking while talking to police. Besides enduring degrading and humiliating treatment such as strip searches (including anal cavity searches in which some officers enjoy probing with their fingers), I have also endured physical abuse by officers and jailers. I had one Ada county sheriff's deputy slap the back of my head as I was walking to court in full restraints, belly cuffs and leg shackles. Another pushed me into a cell with such force that I fell smashing my head on the concrete floor. However, what I experienced is nothing compared to what I have witnessed.

I have witnessed county sheriff deputies use excessive amounts of force more times than I can count. I once watched in horrified amazement as three county sheriff deputies beat a young man who was already in restraints, handcuffed behind his back, and then Tasering him again and again. I personally witnessed these three sheriff deputies laughing about it when done. The hurt and abuse I have witnessed at the hands of the county sheriff deputies, the screaming that I heard, the suffering I felt for these men has been forever imprinted in my memory. This abuse is a crime against humanity itself, committed by the very people sworn to uphold our values and laws.

There seems to be no real physical requirements to become an Ada county jailer or an Idaho state correctional officer, other than having a heartbeat. A large number of Idaho's deputies and correctional officers are extremely overweight (literally a cheeseburger away from a stroke or a heart attack). Though the majority are well paid, many deputies and correctional officers are physically unable to do the job taxpayers are paying them to do. They spend their shifts and watches surfing the Internet, often watching porn or playing video games, everything else but there job. Ada county deputies are always on their smartphones listing to music with headphones, paying little attention to what is going on around them. Foul language is widespread; required duties often bring a barrage of complaints and curses. This lack of concern and physical ability puts inmate lives at risk.

The Ada county district attorney's office and the public defender's office share the same office space. Both are in the same building on the same floor. They work side by side with one another and are paid by the same county. The difference is that, while public defenders are underbudgeted, the district attorney's office has an unlimited amount of resources. Public defenders are extremely underpaid when considering the size of their case loads, while deputy prosecutors receive a greater amount of compensation for far fewer cases (county district attorneys are paid more than the district judges). This greater resource enables prosecutors and district attorneys to control the courts and judges by manipulating time frames and the system itself.

My family was always there for support while I was working my way through the court process. They watched and listened as the wheels of justice turned. They witnessed prosecuting attorneys and public defenders hang out and talk shop on the fifth-floor balcony while smoking cigarettes during recess (this is a smoking area at the Ada county courthouse). My family informed me of how they overheard the deputy prosecuting attorney working my case talking shop jargon, bragging about how many felonies they had convicted and how many prison years they had handed out for the week.

My family was beyond frightened to the point of disgust by this conversation. They could not believe what they overheard. The justice system they believed in had nothing to do with justice but was actually a conviction competition. There was no room for right or wrong, unjust sentences, and destroying lives was the goal. Public servants who behave this way have no respect for the law or the community in which they serve. Our laws are just; what makes them unjust are the ones who do not respect them and use their power for personal gain and/or as a weapon.

Our justice system was designed with two sides in mind: the letter of the law and the spirit of the law. A man that poaches a deer or steals crates of food from a delivery truck to feed his starving children should not be punished the same as a wealthy man who commits these same crime for personal monetary gain. Nevertheless, our system has become distorted, and the first man in this scenario is often punished to a greater extent than the second.

Case in point—a teenager from a wealthy family was charged with three counts of vehicular manslaughter after killing three people in a DUI-related accident. His defense attorney argued that he suffered from *influenca* (derived from influence), meaning he was too wealthy to understand what he was doing. The judge agreed, and the teen was released on probation. Another wealthy man, while driving his Bentley, hit a car pushing it into a lake and drowning the driver. The wealthy man fled the scene. Charges were filed after months of public outrage, but nothing became of the case. And let's not forget the purposely manipulated mortgages and following housing market crash of 2008. Not one person was held accountable after ripping off millions of American families. More recently is the Wells Fargo scandal. They stole millions in phony loans and opening unwanted accounts, and what was done about it? An executive resigned with a $124,000,000 bonus. I must admit that I do find it ironic, with all the violence and excessive force used against the African-American population in America, that it was a black man by the name of O. J. Simpson that proved money can buy our criminal justice system.

Not all lawyers are corrupt, worthless, or evil. Not all are looking for personal gain off the backs of the less fortunate. My oldest daughter (my baby girl) is a lawyer (passed the bar exam the first time when she was twenty-seven). I know for a fact that she has integrity and the heart to make a difference in this world by doing what is right, no matter what. However, I have come to the reality that attorneys like my daughter, are a rare oddity.

In my first case, the one with the broken window, my ex-girlfriend, went back to California shortly after my arrest. During this case, the district attorney's office used Idaho tax dollars to pay my ex-girlfriend to come back to Idaho. The district attorney's office paid her airfare (first class) to and from Los Angeles to Boise, Idaho. They also paid for her hotel, car rental, and meals. And they did this twice. This is a common practice by the district attorney's office, paying for their witness to show up in court, to testify for them.

Idaho's population is small (1.5 million); everybody knows everybody in and around the justice system, and no one wants to step on anyone's toes (the Good Ol' Boy system). I had one public defender say to me, "Do not embarrass me in the courtroom." I was appalled; I could not believe my ears. I did not know how to react or what to say and ended up saying nothing, not out of fear of embarrassing him but out of fear of what he might do to my case.

I was appointed seven different public defenders during my last case when I violated a no-contact order by calling home to my wife. During sentencing, as part of a plea deal arranged by my public defender and the prosecuting attorney, I was forced to sign a waiver giving up my right to appeal. I said nothing as I signed the waiver, not wanting to embarrass my public defender. I truly regret doing so; I truly regret being so uninformed and timid. I thought that was why we had public defenders, to protect us and our rights. I have come to know now that signing that waiver both the prosecuting attorney and my public defender got away with misconduct by forcing me to admit to a crime that I did not do, intimidating of a state's witness by third party. Why would I need to sign this waiver if not to hide their misconduct?

The Idaho Department of Corrections staff is divided, separated into different job positions. The majority are correctional officers who deal and interact directly with inmates on a daily basis. There is also administration—education and medical personnel who work in and around the prison facilities. Many are overworked and underpaid while others have become calloused and do as little as possible, not doing the job duties that they were hired to do. The latter have become part of the prison problem. Idaho's prison staff is usually not as violent as the Boise Police or the Ada county sheriff's department, but the discontent is still there.

I am sure working conditions and environment play a large role in the discontent. Though I have heard the state benefits are good, shifts are long (twelve hours), pay is usually low, and there is constant power struggles with not just inmates but coworkers as well.

As an inmate's time grows short, they are required to fill out a questionnaire packet and then meet with an officer of the State of Idaho Commission of Pardons and Parole. This meeting is referred to as their *pre-board hearing*. The hearing officer's job is meeting with inmates to make sure the packet is completely filled out and the parole board has all the right information about them. The pre-board officer will then submit this information to the board with a recommendation, and inmates are then scheduled to see the board (some inmates, depending on crimes committed, do not have to appear before the board, but a determination will be made based on the paperwork submitted by the pre-board officer).

(The Parole Board or, as it is known to most inmates, the Sentence Adjustment Committee). There, inmates wishing to be granted parole will be asked questions and a determination will be made based on several factors: the type of crime, past arrest record, institutional history, past parole history, and community support and housing. Though this seems like a fairly straightforward process; as with any bureaucracy, it has a tendency to become muddled.

Unfortunately, arrest records are often misleading and/or misinterpreted. Even when charges have been dismissed, they remain on your arrest record, and when trying to explain this fact, it is taken as not taking accountability for your actions. This misleading information is often passed on to the parole commission by your pre-board officer and used against you during your parole hearing. And up to this point in my prison career, I have been denied parole four different times. And I'm what IDOC considers as being a perfect inmate never causing any problems with prison staff; I keep my mouth shut and always did what I was told without any argument, yet it meant nothing to the parole commission.

The parole board confines people not for offenses they have committed but for crimes they might commit in the future. The parole board uses an un-realistic criteria to determine whether he or she is deemed more likely than not to re-offend. Making it virtually impossible for anyone to meet the parole boards criteria. This un-realistic criteria is just a guessing game, and it's unprofessional, especially when there are so many lives involved. Parole boards are vested with almost unlimited power to decide who gets out of prison, when and why. Parole boards are vested with almost unlimited discretion to make decisions on almost any basis—hearsay, rumor, and instincts are all fair game.

President Obama has made comments regarding Idaho's mass incarceration, and the federal government is fully aware that Idaho is hoarding inmates for profit. The leading factor to this hording is Idaho's Commission for Pardons and Parole. The parole commission has no rules or regulations to follow. They are appointed directly by the governor and do whatever they choose, answering only to the corrupt governor. There are no requirements or qualifications to become a parole commissioner. To my knowledge, not one of the current commissioners has any experience with the justice system what so ever. Idaho's unregulated parole commission is one of the leading factors to why the prison system remains full beyond capacity.

There was talk of doing away with the parole board as other states have done, but apparently, Butch Otter could not have his overly paid friends in the unemployment lines. Politicians, who are bound by open records and disclosure laws and are accountable to their constituents, parole boards often operate behind closed doors and wield so much power.

During my November 7, 2016, hearing (my last sentence adjustment hearing), I was asked if I believed in God and what religion I followed. Shocked by the question, I simply answered that I did and gave my religious preference. Now that I have had time to think about this, I cannot help but wonder if I was denied parole because I gave the wrong religious belief. Be it as it may, though I didn't know of it then (clue-less) but I do now. And for those who don't know; Idaho is a Mormon state. Mormons control Idaho's politics, unfortunately there is no separation between church and state. Regardless I obviously gave the wrong religious following (my bad).

The pre-board officer whom I had met with must have been in a rush because the report that went in front of the parole commission was full of inaccuracies. There were numerous errors, including wrong dates and even wrong charges. The board believed I had been arrested for possession of methamphetamine and intimidating a state witness. There was no mention of the charges that actually sent me back to prison, violating a no-contact order. The pre-board officer's summary report painted a horrible picture that was not accurate and did not show the true reason I was in front of the board. I tried to answer their question truthfully, but the paperwork they had in front of them said something else; therefore, I was lying. I was then denied parole. I was told to come back in December 2017. However, I have concerns about that date as well. I fear I will be denied parole again because of not only the inaccuracies, but I have been told the system likes trouble-free inmates. I would have never believed the latter about the good inmates a few years ago, but it only makes sense that trouble free inmates are good for their prison business.

Unlike most states, Idaho is a state that sentences convicted criminals to unified prison sentences. Meaning sentences have a mandatory time followed by an indeterminate time to be determined by the parole commission. This means convicted felons only know the least amount of time and the maximum amount of time they are to serve. In other words, they have no idea when they will be released unless they plan to do their entire sentence in prison.

The Idaho parole commission will often deny inmates who have completed their fixed amount of time, requiring inmates to go before the board two to three times before giving them a release date. In most cases, when one does receive a parole date, it may be months or even years before they are released.

I have done years past my fixed time at the expense of the tax-payers. And because of this, not knowing when my family and I will be united, we cannot plan our future. Not knowing when one may be released is torture on the mind, body, and spirit; it truly inflicts havoc on one's well-being. In my last case, between my court-ordered sentence and the parole commission, I was punished five different times for one crime. And it's not over yet, because I am still in prison.

Not only does the Idaho parole board keep convicted felons beyond their court-ordered fixed portions of their sentences, but those violated will have the time done on parole taken from them. Meaning, if a felon was sentenced in 2000 to five years fixed and five indeterminate, for a total of ten years, it does not guarantee his time will be done in 2010. If he does his fixed portion and is released on parole, then violated their parole and then returned to prison, the parole commission restarts the indeterminate portion of that individual's sentence upon their return to prison. This happens over and over and there are a large number of Idaho inmates who end up doing two and even three hundred percent of their sentences.

I know of one man from Hagerman, Idaho, Kyle Cornelison, that was sentenced to a two plus three for a total of five years when he was eighteen. He did two hundred and twenty percent of his sentence, finally topping it out when he turned thirty years old. Idaho took his entire twenties for breaking into a convenience store and taking a few hundred dollars' worth of beer, cigarettes, and steaks.

These are the years of a man's life when they define themselves, when they find a trade, get married, and start families. What kind of people are we as a society creating when we strip these important years from our young over a couple of hundred dollars that was paid back in a few months?

Inefficiencies in the Idaho Department of Corrections and the Idaho State Parole Board have resulted in thousands of prisoners being kept in prison long beyond their parole eligibility dates. The cost of incarcerating inmates two and three hundred percent of their sentences is costing Idaho's taxpayers millions of dollars every month. If Idaho released all inmates when fixed portions of sentences were completed and gave paroled inmates the time they have done on supervised parole (inmates also pay for their supervision), the majority of Idaho inmates would be released from prison today. This would drastically reduce Idaho's prison population and save tax payers tens of millions of dollars each and every year. I also contend that releasing these inmates would not affect Idaho crime rates in any way. We have to ask ourselves, what is preventing this common-sense solution? Could it be Idaho's elite want to protect their cash cow, their prison industry?

Not unsurprisingly, states with higher incarceration rates, like Idaho, also have a higher number of people on Probation and Parole. National statistics show that those exiting prison on Probation and Parole in 2014, that over a third failed to successfully complete their supervision. Idaho's statistics are even higher, almost three times the national average at 85 percent recidivism.

If you are lucky enough to be granted parole, you must sign a Conditions of Parole contract before being released. This contract lists all conditions set by the parole board with the exception of one line, which states you agree to comply with any additional conditions and restrictions your assigned parole officer may stipulate. Once released, you are to report to the probation and parole office in your assigned district within twenty-four hours. You may or may not meet with your parole officer at that time. More often than not, after this initial check-in, you will be required to report in by phone every day until your assigned parole officer has time to see you. When you do meet with your parole officer, you will be required to sign another copy of your conditions of parole, which may contain additional conditions set by your parole officer.

Because Idaho's probation and parole officers are overloaded with infinite numbers of caseloads, they are often unable to make personal connections with those in their care and end up violating those who really should not be violated. Case in point, a man gets laid off from work due to no fault of his own. Money is tight and he is having trouble paying bills, including his cost of supervision. Other life situations become difficult, kids need school clothes, and his wife is getting on him or whatever. Though this man knows it will only make matters worse, it is the only escape he has ever known and he uses. He needs help, but since his parole officer has no real idea what is going on in his life, and he failed a drug test, he is violated and sent back to prison (remember, IDOC teaches that relapse is part of recovery). Even if he is not sent back to prison, he will have to do additional classes and parole checks, making finding and holding a job nearly impossible.

My personal experience with probation and parole has also been mixed, both good and bad. The last parole officer I had seemed to be a good man, he was polite and respectful to me (something I have been told is an oddity). However, due to the fact he was overworked, having hundreds of parolees on his case load, he became frustrated and quit the job. I went seven months without a parole officer, and during that time, I called probation and parole office weekly, questioning why I didn't have a parole officer, and no one could give me an honest answer.

However, the first parole officer I had was very controlling. I would have a set time to come in to the P&P office for my parole checks, but I would still end up waiting hours past my scheduled time. My employer became frustrated, and I lost a good job because of this. Everything was at her convenience; my life revolved around her. This became overbearing and stressful for me; jobs are very hard to come by for ex-cons but especially hard while on probation or parole.

Some parole officers' caseloads are so large and overwhelming that they reduce their case loads by violating clients for anything and everything. A dirty drug test will send a person back to prison (again, IDOC teaches that relapse is part of recovery). I had a bunkie that was violated for gambling. He had bought some lottery tickets and this parole officer said that playing the Idaho lottery was gambling. Many people are sent back to prison for being late on their cost of supervision payments (COS or, as known by parolees, state extortion payments), even when parole officers are aware they have yet to find work.

I have also seen probation and parole officers around town doing personal business on what looked to be taxpayers' time. While applying for a job at a car lot, I watched one officer test drive two separate vehicles as his partner waited in a state-owned SUV. Another time, at a cell phone store, I witnessed a parole officer upgrading to a newer phone, and again his partner was browsing around the store. I also found a coffee house that I liked to frequent, and just about every time I went there, there would be a handful of parole officers hanging out. I realize these officers work grueling hours and cama-raderie is important, but it did little to calm my aggravation when thinking of the countless hours I spent waiting in the probation and parole office for my parole officer. Sure, they could have been on a break or off the clock, but it did not look that way to me. It looked very much like they were wasting tax dollars and not doing the job that they were hired to do. Perception is everything.

The truth, I believe Idaho's media outlets such as newspapers, televisions, and radio news outlets are being manipulated into ignoring the truth. These organizations do not tell the entire truth purposely leaving out valuable information. And I believe, these media outlets especially here in Idaho purposely down play situations, and leave out facts when it comes to Idaho's prison business for profit to its county jails and its justice system due to fear, what else could it be for not reporting corruption and the waste of tax dollars. Innocence until proven guilty is a farce; they convict the accused in the public eye before the trial. Normal well-intentioned or hard-nosed jour-nalists, they tend to take statements by public officials, government officials, and prison officials at face value, with no type of critical disbelief. This is not journalism—it's favoritism. When watching the news or reading the paper, one should always remember to be weary of half-truths; you might be fed the wrong half.

Everyone who works for our justice system—police officers, sheriff deputies, judges and courtroom clerks, correctional officers, parole commissioners, probation and parole officers, and every other public servant—has the opportunity to make a difference in this world if they choose to. These are the people our children look up to, and they should be held to a higher standard of morality. The behavior of our public servants should always promote right living and do so by leading by example. It is crucial for all to teach, prepare, and motivate right living no matter whom or what you do for a living, but even more so for those public servants that our children look up to. The future and moral well-being of America's children depends on it.

However, when a crime is committed against a police officer, the penalty doubles for the person committing that crime. Yet when one of our public officials commits a crime, they are usually penalized less than the average citizen. Why is that? As mentioned in chapter 4, an Idaho deputy sheriff was charged with a misdemeanor, child endangerment, after violently throwing a handicapped toddler across a room, killing the child. He was sentenced to six months' work release, which was to be served at a nearby fire department (a twenty-four-hour facility). The sentencing judge stated that his public service was the determining factor in his sentencing. Public outrage later forced the deputy to finish his last few months in the Gooding county jail, where, though he did sleep in the jail at night, he was allowed to drive around with Gooding County patrol officers during the day.

This is an outrage! It is my sincere belief that anyone that has the capability to abuse a toddler would also abuse the power of their position in life. How many others suffered at the hands of this abuser? I also contend that these servants should be held to an even higher standard of law as well as morality then those they serve. Our public servants need, and should be held accountable when they fail to do the job that the tax payers are paying them to do! They need to be held to a higher standard, they are America's role models, our children look up to these types of people. These people have an impact on so many lives, what they do directly affects everybody, you and me on a daily basis.

Ask yourself this question: are the public servants in your area doing the job that the taxpayers are paying them to do? Truth is, the majority of citizens are clueless of what is going on in their community. The public has right to know whether elected judges or public servants are performing their duties competently and ethically while in office, and yet this information is a secret, hidden away from the public eyes.

I will say again, it is crucial for all to teach, prepare, and motivate no matter what their position in life, no matter who one is or what one may do for a living. However, our children look up to those public servants wearing badges, as they should, and it is crucial that our public servants behavior be that of promoting right living by leading by example. The future of American children depends on it. It is also crucial that our opinions be voiced. Collective voices have incredible power. It was the resonating voices of the world that brought down the Berlin Wall, and resonating voices that freed Nelson Mandela. And it is our collective voices that can and will make the desperate change needed in our American justice system and accompanying prison industry.

CHAPTER 14

Idaho's True Colors, its Dark Side

To better understand Idaho's true colors, its dark side let's rewind to previous problems I have exposed. We are already aware that President Obama and the federal government understands and recognize Idaho as being a carceration state, a state imprisoning their citizens for profit. We know that Idaho's governor, Butch Otter, throughout his political career has maintained financial relations with the private prison industry operating not only in Idaho but within other states Idaho inmates were being housed. Please don't let me forget to remind you that Governor Otter openly discriminated against same sex marriages. And he wasted tax dollars doing so while trying to prevent same sex equality here in Idaho. I believe Otter's behavior was personal and far from professional. I say shame on him and I have mentioned how Idaho is being ripped off by public servants not doing the jobs that the taxpayers are paying them to do.

I have mentioned how abusive and damaging the justice system is, imprisoning our youth, by creating monsters who become criminals for life at the expense of the tax payer, and creating and producing future criminals for life who are now homosexual. I have informed you of the twisted sexual practices going on behind the walls and of how many young men are leaving prison after obtaining

AIDS and continuing these perverted practices or, at best, a homo-sexual life style. I have also made it clear that Idaho has a serious drug problem within the walls of its jails and prison system and that heroin and its opiate friends are on the rise, destined to destroy Idaho's youth in years to come. I have talked of the brutality and violence within the walls of Idaho's jail and prisons, of how little is being done to help prevent these brutal atrocities.

It would be unfair if I didn't remind you of the high population of registered and unregistered sexual predators being released into Idaho communities every day. Individuals so perverted that I have known some that would tattoo themselves with diapers to brag of their victims (I was stuck in a cell with a sick freak that had thirteen diaper tattoos on his forearm, one for each of his victims). I have also addressed the manipulation of treatment programs and of how this manipulation will fail Idaho, costing billions as education (the real solution to recidivism) takes a back seat.

Everything I have mentioned is documented; it is public knowledge and it is well known of by those in power. The sad truth is the news media has a large role in hiding these truths. They have ignored the men and women behind the walls after exploiting them during arrest processes and ongoing court proceedings. They are directly fed these stories by police and prosecutors wanting to raise public outrage and secure their chances of conviction. The media submits to this deception to improve ratings, which in turn creates greater income through the sale of advertising time. Misery loves company, and people watch and talk about these stories. As always, there is a money trail. This without any question is deception, being influenced because of corruption.

Yet Idaho has a much deeper dark side, a side that I have come to see since arriving in Idaho, racial discrimination. Idaho's population is predominantly all white. Northern Idaho is famously known for having many white supremacy compounds, and there has been several racially charged incidents in and around these hate group compounds. And I'm sure you know about the Ruby Ridge incident here in Idaho. (2017 was the 25th anniversary of what happened there at Ruby Ridge). Idaho was also a destination for confederate sympathizers before and after the civil war of the 1860s. Many of Idaho's towns still carry the names given by confederate sympathizers such as Dixie and Atlanta, names of common cities in the south.

There is a famous saying commonly known in Idaho: "If you ain't white, you ain't right."

This saying is no joke. Idaho breeds and teaches hate, especially against all who are not white. The most resent showing of this hate was in the town of Mountain Home (home of the Mountain Home Air Force Base), about forty-five miles south of Boise. An African-American high school girl paid to decorate a parking space, choosing a depiction of herself with the caption, *Black Lives Matter*. A large number of upset white residents protested this young girl's depiction, chanting all lives matter as they waved confederate flags (a symbol of heritage, not of hate, so they claimed). To prove they did not hate, the all-white protesters brought the group of counter protesting high school students' watermelon and fried chicken.

I am not a person of color but pride myself in looking past color and only seeing people as people (I have often marked *Other* on applications that ask my race, believing I am of the human race). My time in Idaho has been a nightmare, and when adding the ugliness of discrimination and hate, it has somehow left me feeling dirty, as if I need to shower from simply walking among those who openly express this rhetoric.

Once I went to prison, I was then forced to associate and live with people who love to hate all who are not like them, all who are not white (it is overwhelming for me to be around such mongers of hate). Idaho prisons are full of white gangs and hate groups (Aryan Knights, Aryan Brotherhood, Skin Heads, and other white supremacy groups—Mexican gangs make up the rest). Unfortunately, not all of those who hate are inmates. Over the years, I have notice county sheriff's deputies IDOC correctional officers with gang and hate group affiliation tattoos such as the number 88, 13 and SS (lightning bolts). Not cool, how is this not a security or safety issues? A correctional officer in Cottonwood prison in Northern Idaho, was arrested on a statutory rape charge. When officers raided his home, they found a large amount of illegal munitions. They also found he was affiliated with a militia group, a white supremacy militia group. The munitions charges were conveniently dismissed, but he was sentenced to prison time for the statutory rape, and a prisoner swap was made with Washington State.

In all my years of being locked up in Idaho, I have seen only three black sheriff deputies working at the Ada county jail, and one black female citizen working in the kitchen. There was a fourth black male deputy who was physically assaulted by another Ada county sheriff's deputy, who, by the way, was white. After the assault, the black deputy was forced into early retirement by his white superiors (allegedly).

I mentioned in an earlier chapter of witnessing county sheriff's deputies' use of Tasers, two of those three incidents I witnessed involved black men, and one of those men was restrained in handcuffs. I have personally heard Ada county sheriff deputies use racial degrading words, calling black men *niggers* and *monkeys*. I have witnessed other inmates as well as jail and prison staff openly displaying their hate against all who are not white; their hate does not stop at only black men. I have seen Ada county sheriff deputies and prison staff (IDOC) cozying up with hate groups (white gang members). I have seen firsthand how black, Mexican, Asian, Muslim, and Native American men are being treated behind the walls of Idaho, and it is far from fair or right!

There are approximately ten black men (probably less) in the Idaho prison I was housed in, and again I have only seen three African Americans who worked for IDOC in all the years I've been incarcerated here in Idaho. I wonder why this is. I have seen how county jail and the Idaho prison system keep black inmates separated from one another. I find it sad and embarrassing that in this day of age, a hundred and fifty years from the Jim Crow era, that hate and bigotry still lives and thrives in states like Idaho. This hate spewing from Idaho's countryside goes beyond race. Idaho's hatred is not simply reserved of men of color, the majority of Idahoan's carrying this hatred are equally hateful toward newcomers. They feel outsiders have created all of Idaho's problems. They blame others for their problems, especially people from California.

There are many in Idaho who despise and blame Californians for everything. I know—I came from California and I am reminded of this every day. It seems half of Idaho's population believes people from California are the ones bringing the drugs and all drug-related crimes; the other half blame the Mexican migrant workers they depend on to harvest their crops. Idahoans are resentful of Californians retiring to Idaho, selling their high-priced estates in California and buying the cheaper-priced homes Idaho has to offer. Of course these same people will tell you they believe in free enterprise and that a man has the right to better himself. They also fail to recognize the money generated by out of state incomes coming into their state as they wallow in their hatred.

This hatred is fed and generated by stupidity, their lack of education and understanding (Idaho is next to last in public education) Idaho public servant's would rather waste tax dollars in its prison business then invest in the children of Idaho future, their education. The uneducated population of Idaho is easily misled and controlled by their corrupt leadership, educated people who twist words like *Right to Work* and *No Child Left Behind.* Everyone believes they have a right to work and no one wants to think of a child left behind. However, Idaho's leadership used this play on words to trick Idahoans into voting in the union busting Right to Work bill by making them believe the bill supports their right to work in Idaho. In all actually, they were voting away their guaranteed union benefits (competitive wages, cost of living increases, health care, retirement, etc.).

Idaho's leadership did the same thing with the No Child Left Behind bill. As I have stated, no one wants to think of a child left behind and the people were once again tricked into voting on a bill that actually hurt our children. Idaho schools started being funded on the performance of students instead of student attendance, which sounds meaningful, and I believe probably started out as so (I have to believe, I cannot accept the fact that others put money ahead of children). Nevertheless, as with everything to do with funding (money) and our bureaucracy, it became twisted. Students that fell behind started being forced out of our public schools in order to improve the school's overall performance. People were purposely manipulating this system in order to gain funding. Idaho schools were no longer leaving students behind; they were leaving them out. And what do you think happens to a child that is left out? Incarceration of course. This is greed and corruption at its worst.

Obviously Idaho's colors do not run striped in red, white, and blue. Its true colors are of greed and hate toward everything, unless it is the dirty green of money. Hate against another human being because of their race, ethnicity, gender, or religion is a behavior that is completely disrespectful to God himself and against humanity, and I refuse to take any part in it. There can be no price put on life, and life is far too short to carry hate in one's heart.

For now, I just sit in prison and wait for my day, and with each day, I pray for all who are sick with hate in their hearts. For now all I can do is write, try to make all aware of what really drives the grinding wheels of mass incarceration. The cure for this sickness lies within the education of our children; they are our true future.

CHAPTER 15

Money

One of the easiest, most universal, and yet most effective ways to draw attention to the issue of mass incarceration is to write about how much money it costs. People do not realize the scope of money involved. Everything I have come to learn and understand about the justice system and how the Prison for Profit business operates can be summed up in one word: *money*. That is all I hear about, and it is all everyone ever talks about. They are not concerned with prison safety or how to reduce recidivism, encouraging family contact, keeping people out of jail and prisons—it's literally all about the money.

We have all heard the old adage "Money makes the world go around," and nowhere is that more true than in the prison industry. Money breeds corruption within the prison for profit industry. It is the number one cause of corruption. It is the root to all that is evil in the lucrative Prison for Profit business. To better understand this corruption and greed, we have to follow the money.

The prison population in the United States was 217,000 in 1963; it now stands at approximately 2.3 million. Of the more than 2.3 million prisoners held in the state and federal facilities at the end of 2015, around 8 percent were housed in private prisons, Correction Corporation of America (CCA) and GEO group alone, took in a combined $3.3 billion in gross revenue in 2014. Correction Corporation of America's gross revenue in 2015 was $1.79 billion and with a net income of around $220 million. The average cost to taxpayers for incarcerating federal prisoners within these companies is $28,893.40 per year, with the average cost for state prisoners between, $125 and $150 per day. Other companies, including Management and Training (MTC), Community Education (CEC), Corizon and Aramark, La Salle Southwest Correction, and Emerald Correctional Management, are privately held and do not make their financial data publicly available.

The Tennessee-based CCA and GEO group are traded on the New York stock exchange. GEO Group bills the federal government about $160 per day to house each immigrant detainee, other contractors, including CCA charge even more. GEO group political action committee alone had donated more than $100,000 to local, state, and federal candidates during the 2014 elections cycle. Both CCA and the GEO group also have spent millions of dollars lobbying on the federal level, including for causes on immigration-related issues to help keep their private prisons full and their pockets stuffed with money.

For the past four decades, our country has relentlessly expanded the size of our criminal justice system allowing private prison companies to reap tremendous profit from human misery. If the Department of Justice released all nonviolent offenders today, it would save taxpayers an estimated $16.9 billion dollars per year. Why do we allow the corruption and greed of those who have an invested interest in private prison industry continue to waste human lives and taxpayers' money?

Private prisons depend solely on incarceration to make their cash, by the billions. Do you really think they want people to do well after they get out of prison, think again. More people and high recidivism rates mean more profit. In July 2015, CCA issued approximately 117 million shares of stock with a market cap of $4.05 billion, while GEO group had issued around 75 million shares with a market cap of $2.76 billion. Stockholders can be anyone, local, state, or federal lawmakers. Many correction officials, judges, and other public employee hold stock in the prison for profit industry. Members of Congress receive huge campaign donations from private prisons (how is this not a conflict of interest?). It is morally repugnant and a national tragedy that America's justice system is being influence by private prisons to keep their beds full. Obviously America's justice is for sale; the questions are "How much?" and "Who is getting paid?" This is truly a colossal waste of human life, all because of a dollar.

As I have previously mentioned, Idaho's prison industry is one of the largest employers of Idaho's citizens. There are a lot of people depending on these jobs. Nevertheless, it does not make it right for the justice system to abuse its authority and power to keep the wheels turning for a profit. Idaho's prison population exploded after agreeing to allow CCA to set up camp within Idaho's borders. When such contracts are agreed upon, bed quotas are made, and quickly, money changes hands in the way of campaign contributions. These types of contracts are infamous across the United States when states do business with private prisons. According to experts, states become obligated against their communities' best interests, keeping prisons filled to ensure that the taxpayer dollars aren't being wasted. Where there are incentives to keep the private prisons full, it is reducing the likelihood that states will not adopt strategies to reduce prisons' cost by keeping more people out. Private prisons have a much higher recidivism. Keeping people out of prison would obviously be bad for business.

The notion of special interest having influences on the legislative process that private prisons money influences pro-private prisons in states with mass incarceration is indeed the very definition of corruption. Public servants who accepted bribes, kickbacks, and help funnel citizens through jails and prisons to keep beds full are criminals and need be held accountable. Locking people up to fill beds quotas takes the justice out of our justice system. Kickbacks in the way of campaign contributions or any other way are bribes, and that is corruption.

Corrections Corporation of America (CCA) is the largest for-profit prison firm in the United States. The Department of Justice (DOJ) announced in August 2016 that it plans to eliminate its use of privately operated facilities to house federal prisoners, which sparked a sharp decline in CCA's stock price. DOJ's decision to phase out private prisons resulted in 40 percent drop in CCA market value. After the DOJ's decision, in October of 2016, CCA announced they were to change names to Core Civic. However, no matter what they call themselves, the company business model remains the same, to make money by not spending enough to provide safe, secure facilities and adequate medical care for prisoners who are in their care. Changing of name is admission of failure that cost taxpayers billions and ruined many lives.

From the very first day of arrest, American citizens are financially exploited and extorted by the justice system. Not just the one arrested but their family and friends as well. County jails are much more than simply jails. Jails have become local businesses by exploiting and extorting citizens in any way possible for profit. Idaho's Ada county jail, where I was housed, is no exception; it's a money-making machine abusing their authority and its power for profit. And if you're a person without means (indigent), you will go without soap and other hygiene necessities. You will also go hungry, and you will go without communication with the outside world. Though indigent inmates will be furnished two envelopes a week, the use of phones to call for help, to a friend or family is reserved for those with incoming funds. And those with incoming funds are exploited at mind-boggling rates.

Over the last decade, the phone business has become a scandalous industry, characterized by many lawsuits, exorbitant fees, high phone rates and monopolistic relationships between jails, prisons and private companies that openly offer kickbacks to jailers and prisons facilities. County jails and prison phone calls are notoriously expensive for inmates and their families, rates as high as $17.30 for a fifteen-minute phone call. Their family and friends are charged a service fee to set up inmate accounts at the jail or prison. Then they are charged a fee every time they add money to the account (wireless administration fee and payment processing fees). And in most cases, additional charges are added for a separate account just for the use of the phones. When one takes into account all the additional charges and fees, a ten-dollar amount would give on average, about four and a half to five and a half dollars on an inmate's account. This is no more than blackmail or highway robbery, and this type of robbery doesn't stop there.

While I was being held in the Ada county jail, I was paying $4.50 to call my mother outside of Boise Idaho, yet I was paying $5 to call my wife who lived inside of Boise where the jail is located. And remember, these phone calls were only fifteen minutes long. This is abusive, discriminatory, and unreasonable.

Prisons and jails get a commission from the revenues generated by inmate phone calls. Prison and jail communications throughout the United States generate 1.5 billion dollars a year in profits, all paid for by the human misery of incarceration, off the backs of the poor and unfortunate. The prison phone industry is rife with greed, shamelessly profiting and exploiting vulnerable consumers. The phone industries executives have openly colluded with correctional professionals to milk billions of dollars from prisoners and their family and friends. Many families are isolated because they have no money to pay such high phone rates and it's the children who are paying the high price when they go without contact of a parent (now that's a true crime). My question is, where is all this money going? Who is receiving these kickbacks and bribes, especially here in Idaho, the millions, where is this money?

Extorting inmates and their family and friends are a common practice in the prison business and it doesn't stop at phone calls. Phones are only the tip of the profiteering iceberg, only the beginning of these crimes. Communication is more than just a phone. Modern communication can be electronic (e-mails and video). County jails and prisons, normally through the same companies who provides phone service for these institutions. Are now providing inmates with the use of iPads, tablets to use to send e-mails. Inmates may also listen to music, play video games, and watch videos, movies, or porn right in the comfort of their bunk or in their cell, at a price per minute of course. Billions of dollars are being made from this new technology as well. This provides a whole new source of income for jails and prisons. Again I ask, "Where this money going?" who is receiving these lucrative kickbacks.

Another form extortion and robbery used throughout America's jails and prisons is by the way of commissary stores. Commissary stores provide inmates the opportunity to purchase hygiene, writing material and stamps, food, and a small amount of clothing items at overly inflated prices (of course). Commissary contracts are awarded to the lowest bidder, meaning whoever can give the biggest kickbacks. The two largest vendors are Keefe, headquartered in Sparks, Nevada, and Mid-States, out of Texas. All prisons have the option of using a pre-packaged service where inmates' orders are packaged at the vendors' headquarters before being shipped or the vendors sell in bulk and uses cheaper prison labor to package orders, creating more revenue for both the vendors and the prison.

Though Idaho's prison system uses Keefe to provide commissary to prison inmates, Idaho county jails have no uniformity, using different vendors and sometimes doing their own commissary. Ada County is allegedly running its own commissary store in hopes of generating more profits. But who is reaping in these profits?

Obviously, commissary venders like Keefe and Mid-States who buy and supply for millions of detainees have the buying power to obtain items such as a price of a ramen noodles at a lower cost than Ada County, creating near-equal profit margin. So one would have to ask, why a jail such as Ada County would choose to do their own commissary store (allegedly). Unless it was easier to channel money into the pockets of those in charge? I have no evidence of this, but one does not need a degree in economics to know that specialized companies such as Keefe and Mid-States can and do provide commissary services cheaper than a few of uncaring guards at a county jail can. All one has to do to verify this fact is talk to the county jails that do use these specialized services.

In any case, whether using specialized vendors or not, prices are highly inflated, causing human suffering for not only those behind bars but putting a financial burden on the families of inmates as well. Price gouging is criminal outside the walls of American institutions and should be on the inside as well.

In recent times, jail administrators have found a new revenue stream, exploiting prisoners' addiction to nicotine by selling them electronic cigarettes, or e-cigarettes, for a substantial profit with profit margins as high as 400 percent, and most jails are now charging inmates as high as fourteen dollars to have another inmate cut their hair. Their excuse is, they need money.

Out of the 2.3 million people locked up in the United States at any given time, around 646,000 are held in county jails. Seven out of ten pre-trial detainees who have not yet been found guilty must remain in jail because they cannot afford to make bond (bail), and the longer people stay in the jails, the more money the jails make (at the expense of the taxpayer) and more likely the accused is to accept a plea deal to resolve their charges. This is mass-incarceration for profit (text book) that helps create revenue for the county, and taxpayers are being extorted and manipulated into paying this unnecessary bill. Due to this abuse of power for profit by your local politician who by the way are giving themselves pay raise at your expense as often as they can, ask yourself this have I ever seen a poor politician? (There are no poor politicians). Prosecutors notoriously (especially here in Idaho) abuse their authority by setting extremely high bonds just to keep the wheels of injustice turning for profit at the expense of human life and the American taxpayer.

Studies show the weight of the criminal justice system falls heavily upon the poor and minorities and the mentally ill. Idaho, for one, has no real funding for the mentally ill and has resorted to locking them up and putting them on medication, including our military veterans suffering PTSD and other illnesses cause by their service to our country.

Our Constitution guarantees the accused the presumption of innocence until being proven guilty, that rings are especially hollow for those that cannot afford bond. Though I am sure our forefathers meant the presumption of innocence until being proven guilty as a *per se* exigency, throughout the United States, the new deathly hollow ring is "Guilty until proven innocent." Many low-income citizens can simply not afford the additional expenses of paying for a bond.

In many cases, this expense would mean losing their homes, and their families would go hungry.

High bonds help keep county jails full and, in return, helps them extort the families of those incarcerated. This abusive activity destroys families and ruins lives. According to the Justice Police Institute, the average bail for a person with a felony charge in a large urban area rose by $30,000 from 1992 to 2006. In 2017, Idaho's average is over $100,000 for a felony bond. As the bail amounts continue to rise, pre-trial release rates have gone down. In 1990, 65 percent of felony defendants were released while awaiting trail compared to 58 percent in 2006. According to Pre Trail Institute Study, African-Americans bail average 35 percent higher than white with similar charges. Latino's bail was 15 percent higher.

The United States has the highest incarceration rate in the world, six times that of Canada, China, or Iraq. While the United States has approximately 5 percent of the world's population, it incarcerates 25 percent of the world's prisoners. Incarceration rates in the United States have increased by 700 percent since the 1970s. The total number of Americans under correctional control is seven million or more than one in fifty United States citizens. And did you know that incarceration of juveniles has skyrocketed over the years and it takes an average $88,000 per year to incarcerate a young person in a state facility, more than eight times the amount we invest in their education? The United States is also the only country that allows juveniles to be sentenced to life without parole.

A US Department of Justice report had found that the number of prisoners in states facilities increased by fifty-five percent from 857,000 in 1993 to 1,325,300 in 2013. However, it is the over-fifty-five category that states prison's population have exploded during that same time period, up 400 percent. The large increase in elderly prisoners has resulted in more and more tax dollars because they are often in need of more mental health services, medication, and more specialty medical visits outside the prisons they are being warehoused in. They also need more nursing hours. They need more of everything. The increase of older inmates is a direct result of oversentencing, an abusive justice system locking up a large number of people for petty crimes that should be considered misdemeanors.

In 2006, a report from the Bureau of Justice estimated that 75 percent of women and 63 percent of men incarcerated suffered from some form of mental illness. These types of illnesses go untreated and cost taxpayers at the end of the day more money in the long run. Why? Because their illnesses are not being treated while they are incarcerated because it's cheaper this way then again it's not. There are about 1.25 million people suffering from mental health problems in American prisons and jails, US jails and prisons have become a dumping ground for the mentally ill, and they are being exploited by the justice system. At some point, we have to stop putting ones who are ill in prison and reserve the cells for the worst of the worst kinds of people, the violent murderers and rapists and child molesters, people who are worthy of being in prison.

Though crime is down in the United States, incarceration spending measures skyrocketed to $1.1 trillion. Federal budgets passed by Congress in January 2014 will ensure that many law enforcement agencies receive more funding (a pay increase). FBI will receive $8.3 billion, an increase of $247.7 million over the fiscal year of 2015, and the Federal Bureau of Prisons will receive an $6.77 billion an increase of $90.2 million and the Bureau of Alcohol, Tobacco, Firearms, and Explosives will get a pay raise in their budget of $1.18 billion, more than $49 million over last year.

Research is abundantly clear that post-secondary education and training are greatly needed, having tremendous effectiveness and saves you the taxpayers' money, while at the same time producing productive members of society. We, the people, can help make a difference by questioning our leadership and their motives. We have a choice: reduce crime and save money or suffer increased crime and spend more money.

It is not surprising that finding employment and independence after leaving prison is extremely difficult, especially without any education. Many convicted felons released are undereducated and have few job skills, making it virtually impossible to function in today's technology-based society. Due to a lack of funding, academic and occupational programs in America prisons have declined significantly over the past twenty years, while overall spending on corrections have exploded along with the prison population. According to Emory University's Department of Economics, prisoners who complete some high school recidivate at an average rate of 55 percent with vocational training, recidivism falls to 20 percent, and the rates keep dropping with each additional level of education obtained. Prisoners who earn an associate degree recidivate at a rate of 13.4 percent, while for those who obtain a bachelor's degree, the rate is 5.6 percent. For one earning a master's degree, the rate is effectively 0 percent. Education is more cost-effective in terms of reducing recidivism rates.

Studies show that every dollar spent on prison education saves five or more dollars in corrections expeditors. European Prison Facilities generally strive for rehabilitation rather than retribution by investing more heavily in prisoners' education, leading predictably to far lower rates of recidivism. Investing in prisoners (American citizens, our neighbors) is not merely an ideological imperative; it is also sound fiscal policy. Sadly the United States has more jails and prisons then colleges and universities. Some states, such as Idaho, spends virtually the same amount on prisons as they do on public education, though the amount of students served by far outnumbers the amount of prisoners.

With better education, people are better equipped to find gainful employment, repay debts to society, and become responsible, independent citizens, taxpayers, parents, and most of all, contributors to the community. The United States ended the practice of debtor's prison in 1833. Laws passed ensured the American citizens they could not, and would not, be jailed merely for the crime of being too poor to pay one's debts. Now it seems our justice system has found a back door, bypassing those laws and jailing people for not paying their debts. People who can't pay their court-ordered fines are sent to jail by the court system. This puts the burden on the taxpayer to pay this bill. A person who is sent to jail will sit in jail until the bill is paid by the taxpayer to the local county where this person is being held. How is this practice good business for the American taxpayer?

I am a proud American, but this is not the America I am proud of. No American, no human, should be treated in such a way; it's a slap in the face. Imprisoning people who are too poor to pay court and other legal fees is a violation of our constitutional rights. America is a debtor's prison society, and it's becoming a growing problem here in the home of the free.

Nothing explains the corruption, the greed, and the abuse of power better than Ashtin's story, a man I met while serving my time. Ashtin and I were on the same tier (cell block) at the ISCI (the yard), but because of his missing left leg, I felt uncomfortable talking to him. After several small conversations in chow lines and other places, as I began to know him, I asked about his leg. I had thought I had heard every prison story told, but Ashtin's story surprised even me.

Ashtin was arrested when just eighteen years old for a half an ounce of marijuana. He had been working at a temp service (job placement service) trying to get hired on at a local cheese factory but had been sent out on a construction crew. One of the crewmen also working for the temp service sold marijuana and had asked Ashtin if he wanted to buy some. Ashtin admitted he was no angel and that he had tried marijuana in his past, but besides the fact he had no money for the illegal substance, he had a pregnant girlfriend and was trying to change his life.

After talking with some friends, Ashtin learned that he could make more than fifty dollars if he bought a half ounce for four of his friends to split. Being in desperate need of money, Ashtin told his friends he would do it for them and picked up the half ounce the following day. He had elected to take the marijuana in four different baggies thinking he was doing his friends a favor but was pulled over for failing to come to a full stop after leaving the fellow crewman's house. Canine officers were called and Ashtin was arrested for possession with intent, a felony.

As it turned out, the crewman was a confidential informant and had set Ashtin up. Ashtin was scared and wanted to get out of county jail and support his girlfriend and coming child. He cooperated fully, admitting to everything and agreeing to take a plea bargain for a felony possession. He was sentenced to a two plus three for a total of five years and was put on felony probation.

After awaiting court proceedings and sentencing, Ashtin had spent six months in the county lock up. He and his girlfriend fell desperately behind on all their bills. The added expense of diapers and formula after the birth of his first child, a baby girl, became overwhelming. Trying to catch up the bills was nearly impossible and his cost of supervision was adding up quickly, but his probation officer assured him it would be all right.

A few weeks later, he got a phone message from his probation officer on the answering machine saying they had issued an arrest warrant for his failing to pay cost of supervision (COS). He was told to turn himself in immediately to the sheriff department at the local county jail.

A few days later, there was a loud knock on his door. Ashtin panicked. He knew it was his probation officer; no one else would knock in such an undignified way. He ran through the house and jumped out the upstairs window in the back of the building, breaking his leg as he landed. He hobbled to his car and drove away without being seen, hiding out a week before seeking medical treatment.

After admitting to himself that he needed medical attention and that his escape was futile, he called his probation officer and was immediately taken to the county jail. Though he tried to seek medical attention, weeks went by before jail staff was forced to take notice of his swelling and reddening leg. A bone infection had set in, and Ashtin lost his leg. Shortly after doctors amputated his leg, he was sentenced to prison.

Ashtin was not a bad man but simply a scared kid. He was trying to do right by his girlfriend and daughter but was drawn into temptation by police and their crooked confidential informant, who by the way was allowed to the very thing that Ashtin was arrested for, possessing of marijuana. Police allowed this informant to not only possess marijuana but smoke and sell it in return for information and convictions of the very people he sold to.

However, that is not the end of Ashtin's story. Ashtin got over his fear of going to prison becoming a product of his environment.

He joined a prison gang and started doing illegal drugs within the walls, eventually becoming addicted to heroin. We are talking about a young man who gave up smoking marijuana in order to better himself and support his upstart family.

Ashtin has been in and out of prison ever since. He lost his girlfriend the first time he went to prison; it had been more than fourteen years since he has seen his little girl. When Ashtin first went to prison, the official record stated he was sentenced for possession of a half ounce of marijuana, something that is now legal in eight states and the District of Columbia (Washington, DC) and is also legal for medical use in twenty-five more. However, his violation and what really sent him to prison was being behind on his cost of supervision. How could this be—isn't debtors' prison illegal?

Ashtin is a prime example of how Idaho creates and produces future criminals for life. Ashtin is a product of a carceration state. His crime, though officially it was possession of marijuana, was really about state extortion money, being behind in his cost of supervision.

This situation with Ashtin cost Idaho's taxpayers from the very beginning. It was the taxpayers funding the police and their informant that entrapped Ashtin, setting him up by selling him the marijuana he was arrested for. It was the taxpayers that flipped the bill for his time in county jail, his overworked and underskilled public defender, the prosecuting attorneys, the courts, the judges, the bailiffs, and the jail staff. Taxpayers paid for the amputation of his leg and the special care needed afterwards. The taxpayers are also paying for the public housing his daughter and once girlfriend live in. They have paid for the food stamps and healthcare and every other government benefit handed out to the family Ashtin wanted to support. The taxpayers also pay Ashtin, when not in prison, in the form of Social Security Disability, which, by the way, is far less inexpensive than keeping him in prison.

Ashtin is in his thirties now; he never really had a job other working a few months at the temp service and has never really paid into the tax system. He has also never paid the $360 state extortion money that actually sent him to prison to start with This is not the American dream he dreamed of as a child; those dreams were crushed by our corrupt and greedy justice system. And the sad truth is that this happens over and over throughout our country, to millions of Americans and families wanting only a chance in life. And they say debtor's prison went away back in 1833. Update—six months after I meet Ashtin and learned of his history, I ran into him. He had just got out of the hospital. He told me he went to the dentist to have a tooth pulled, there was some complications and then add incompetence, and he left the dentist chair with a broken jaw. The sad truth is these kinds of mishaps happen all the time, within the walls.

Some economists will argue that labor provided by state inmates not only offsets the cost of housing but is vital to the state's economy. California voters overwhelmingly passed laws to release low-level custody inmates, but state representatives refused, stating California could not afford to release inmates working state jobs. State and federal penitentiaries provide a small army of workers—cheap, coerced by retaliation, and less likely to complain. Nearly a million prisoners are now making office furniture, working in call centers, fabricating body armor, taking hotel reservations, working in slaughterhouses, working in textile manufacturing, and working in the shoe and clothing industry while getting paid pennies a day (many years ago this was called slave labor). Companies like Chevron, Bank of America, AT&T, and IBM are allegedly making super profits from the slave labor of Americas prisoners.

Idaho inmates work many state jobs, benefitting the state but hurting the families of both the inmate working the job as well as the person that should be working that very job. Two families are starving; two families are not paying taxes and contributing to our economy as they should or want to because of this practice. Though it is illegal for prison to make a profit from inmate labor, Idaho inmates also work a number of jobs in the private sector. Approximately one hundred inmates are working for the potato industry in St. Anthony, Idaho. Though the inmates do benefit from this program, this cozy deal reaps huge benefits for the Idaho prison and the potato industry but does little for the inmates themselves. Most, if they are lucky, leave the prison with only a couple thousand after working the worst jobs the industry has to offer for multiple years.

The Idaho penitentiary also runs Correctional Industries (CI) at the Idaho State Correctional Institution (ISCI). There they stamp state license plates and make furniture to be sold to colleges and other state offices. However, they also contract out to the private sector as well. Micron contracts ISCI to wash and package gloves worn by their workers. Inmates working these jobs are paid approximately thirty cents an hour. This is a direct violation of prison labor laws, as well as the labor laws throughout or country. However Idaho has sidestepped these laws by calling the prison's Correctional Industries a program, a job training program. This way there is no need, or rather any law, requiring Idaho's prison industry to pay minimum wage, workman compensation, or state and federal taxes. If an inmate gets hurt, they are quickly replaced with no compensation.

I have come to an ugly truth in my life: I am officially broke. I have no more money in savings. All these years in prison have bled me dry, I have lost everything, and now I am unable to get out of prison because I am broke. I have no money to pay for a halfway house. A majority of Idaho inmates released are forced to go to halfway houses. Halfway houses want the money up front, and in order for me to get out of prison, I must come up with four hundred and fifty dollars, a nonrefundable payment. I have applied for transitional funding, but I was denied and will sit in prison until I am able to raise the funds for my transitional housing. Sadly, if I'm unable to raise this money, I will sit in prison for the next seven years. Having no opportunity to raise these funds has left my future uncertain and will cost Idaho taxpayers hundreds of thousands of dollars. I cannot help but feel a hostage to the system. This is another example how IDOC keeps prison full at tax payers expense.

There are simple solutions to some of the financial burdens of not only Idaho's mass incarceration but throughout all of America. Education and job training are but a couple. The cost of these programs could be offset by simple things like recycling. America's prisons carelessly waste vast amounts of natural resources, many of which could be recycled (paper, plastics, etc.). Tons of food is thrown out of prison kitchens every day, food that could feed the hungry, or if nothing else feed livestock that would in return feed the prison. The ones who are in charge of prison waste must be held accountable, there is no excuses for not recycling. Reduce, reuse, and recycle, I say; it's good for the environment and it's the right thing to do.

Increasing work centers and state-run, not private run, halfway houses would pay for the cost of every inmate living there, that is unless corrupt politicians or officials don't scam off the top. Giving good time alone would save Idaho tax payers millions of dollars per month and it would not increase crime rates in the least.

If Idaho gave inmates good time (time for good behavior) and released all nonviolent offenders when they finished the court-ordered portions of their sentences, it would cut the prison budget in half while at the same time generate additional tax revenue from inmates entering the workforce. In addition to the added revenue and decreased budget, the savings could be diverted to Idaho's floundering school budget, providing better education, creating an improved workforce, and further decreasing prison population. Now that's good business for all of Idaho.

I implore everyone reading this to become proactive. Write your governor and congressmen. Ask why your tax dollars are being wasted on a harsh and outdated prison system that does not work. Ask why we are not taking measures to decrease our spending on prisons while increasing investments in our children's education, our real future.

CHAPTER 16

Mind, Body, and Spirit

A mind is a powerful and beautiful thing, a true gift from God. Unfortunately, many great minds are being wasted behind the walls of America's prisons. I think of the words of John Lennon's song, "Imagine." I imagine a world, living in peace, a world in which people come together to solve problems and life without sickness, without cancer. Now imagine the mind of a child wasting away in a cage, a child with potential to cure cancer, to create peace in the world. Young minds have unlimited potential and should not be wasted, before or after leaving prison.

Not all who go to jail or prison are criminals, ignorant, or lost souls. Imagine someone like Martin Luther King Jr., who was repeatedly jailed, wasting away in a cell instead of leading the civil rights movement of the '60s, or imagine a world in which Nelson Mandela would have remained imprisoned in South Africa. Though these two great individuals were both imprisoned and jailed—Nelson Mandela was even on a United States terrorist watch list until 2008—they are not thought of as criminals or terrorists but remembered for their boldness, their greatness in the face of incredible odds. But imagine if these two individuals were not given a second chance after leaving jail or prison.

The damaging effects of prison can and often do warp a person's mind, and the stigma attached to one when leaving prison can be just as damaging. Many imprisoned, especially the young, never overcome the harmful effects of prison life. They are often denied the opportunity to obtain good jobs, even when they may be the most qualified for the position. Self-esteem is stripped, many fulfilling the words they have heard over and over about themselves; they are worthless and will never change. Good men are often made bad behind the walls of justice.

For me, prison and its aftereffects plays havoc on my mind, body, and spirit. I was in a living hell in my mind and actions. No matter what I did, I couldn't escape, I was trapped, and even more terrifying, no one cared. For a moment in time, I lost my mind, my reality, my sense of what was real. I was seeing things, weird things. When I was in that cage, locked away from all that was real, months at a time without proper nutrition, inadequate amounts of sleep, and a constant mesmerizing buzzing from the fluorescent lamps above my head, never turning off and affecting my very eyesight, my mind began playing tricks on me. When I was locked in the Ada county jail, I didn't see the sunlight or the darkness of night for months. It is no mystery that when forced to live caged as an animal, especially in solitary confinement, one becomes an animal.

The United Nations special rapporteur on torture has described solitary confinement lasting fifteen days or more as constituting a form of torture, and living in such conditions is torture. Being forced to live in solitary confinement, deprived of sleep, nutrition, and sunlight, are all torture techniques used in Nazi Germany, and in recent times. Sadly the Ada county jail have adopted these same mind worping techniques.

One day I turned over to find a new guy in my cage, but the weird thing was, he was not wearing normal jail clothing. He had a reddish kind of glowing complexion, wearing what looked like to be a long leather coat and boots. At the time, I didn't think much of it and turned back over. I was in and out of consciousness and cannot say how long it took to realize something was not right. I rolled over noticing the same guy standing in the same corner of my cage staring at me. As I do with all new cell-mates, I ignored him, quickly turning back over, but thinking to myself how odd it was for him to be wearing a leather coat and boots.

I was hot and miserable in that cage, and yet this guy looked to be cool as an alley cat on a December morning. At that time in my life, I was eating very little, once every other day. As strange and as hard as this is to explain, though I slept periodically all the time, I never felt rested. Between the stress, hunger pains, and lack of real sleep, I was not feeling all that well. I had what seemed to be a never-ending headache; even the back of my eyes hurt. Every night I would lie and think about my day, sinking deeper into depression. My whole world was ending; everything was out of control. I had lost all hope and thought no one cared. I dreamed of saying farewell to it all, lusting for the dull thud of a bullet to end the pain I knew as life.

Every time I heard a sound or got up to use the restroom, there he was, that same freak standing in the corner, never saying a word. His eyes had a strange tint, a glow that was mesmerizing, something that shook my inner core. My anxiety was catching up to me—was this guy for real? And yet, every time I turned around, there he was. Whenever I would wake, I would immediately turn, and now I had found something had changed. For whatever reason, this strange guy was now sitting on the stool, even closer to me.

I jumped up, startled by his closeness, but he just sat there with an evil look on his face, just watching me. I stared back without saying a word, carefully watching him as he was watching me, until I found myself asleep once again. I vaulted from my sleep searching for him, but he was gone. Believing it was a strange dream, I laid back down. When I awoke next, he was back, just sitting there, not saying a word. I felt I was losing my mind, as if I could no longer tell reality from dreams, and began confronting this strange vision. But he just sat unmoving, and I found myself sleeping again.

The next time I awoke, I found him there staring at me again. Enough was enough, I thought, and I started yelling. I cursed him, calling him every name in the book, but he simply sat unmoving. Feeling I had won the battle, I rolled over, still cursing, glancing over my shoulder now and then to let him know I was watching. I awoke again the next day to find him in the same position. I began shouting again, "What do you want with me?" But he never answered.

I cannot remember how long this went on—weeks, maybe months. One night, after noticing he was gone, I decided to piss on that stool he always sat on. I got up and pissed all over it, laughing as I did so. The laughing felt good, something I hadn't done for so long. The next day, I found that son of bitch standing back in the corner wearing an evil grimace, igniting a fear so deep that I do not remember ever being so frightened. As I sat up with my heart pounding, he came at me without moving, as an apparition gliding across the room. He stopped inches from my face, his putrid breath assaulting my every sense. "Do you know who I am?" he questioned.

Startled by his tone, I hesitated. "No."

He moved impossibly closer. "I make dreams come true."

Frightened beyond speaking, I nodded without saying anything. Before I found the courage to respond, he said, "I make dreams come true, and if you keep obsessing about that bullet and wanting to die, I'm the evilness that can make it so."

I scooted back to the corner of my bunk, pulling my postage stamp woolen blanket up around me, and when I looked back up, he was gone. Though beyond scared, what I heard were the realest words I had ever heard, and it was then I understood I had to be stronger and overcome this nightmare. I was obsessing nonstop about that damn bullet, about death. I had a wife and kids, a family who loved me. I knew I had to wake up and see life for what it was. Life was good, life had blessed me, and I knew I wanted to live.

I truly believe my subconscious created that vision to save my life; it was the doing of God himself. I stood solemnly and began cleaning my urine from the floor before staring at my disfigured reflection in the cell's scratched and scarred stainless-steel mirror. Though disheveled from the lack of showering, and weakened by the lack of nutrition, sunlight, and human contact, I could not help but laugh at the thought of someone seeing me laughing out loud while pissing all over the floor. I was actually thankful I didn't have a bunkie because I am sure it would have caused a fight.

I have gone years without adequate amounts of sleep due to my incarceration. There were times I fell asleep while in court to be awakened suddenly and not fully understanding what was going on around me and my surroundings. Since my incarceration, I have not slept longer than an hour at one time. Sleep deprivation constitutes cruel and unusual punishment. According to an article in *Popular Science*, studies have shown that acute sleep deprivation causes mental impairments and can boost hunger-stimulating hormones leading to obesity, while "chronic sleep of five or fewer hours over a ten-year period is associated with a 45 percent elevated risk of heart attack" and increases the likelihood of cancer, heart disease, hypertension, diabetes, stroke, ADHD, alcoholism, and mood disorders. Sleep is extremely important for the overall well-being of all individuals, and it is just as important for those locked in cages.

I believe there are six kinds of insanity. One is doing the same thing over and over again and expecting different results, second is sleep deprivation, third is bipolar disorder, fourth is schizophrenia, and something that I have come to learn and know is depression, and the last is living in fear. For me and many like me, being in prison is living in fear. There are far too many inmates that are living in constant fear for their lives on a daily basis. People who have not been in prison just don't get it—prison is brutal, dehumanizing, and very violent. Throughout my prison time, I was viciously and brutally beaten, and I am traumatized with the memories of each and every one of those beatings. I often smell the breath of that weirdo raping me. I have this ugly picture in my mind of that psychopathic killer I was forced to live with, the look right before he tried to kill me. That look—it haunts my dreams at night. I was traumatized when I witnessed three kids smash another kid's head in—the smell of the blood, the smell, it seems to never go away; that horrible smell makes my stomach sick to this day.

Prison has taken more than my freedom, and I will die before it takes my soul. Over the years, I have struggled with flashbacks and suicidal thoughts. Prison is far from a good mental health environment to live in. There are narcissists, bigots, sadists, and egotistical maniacs, all with terrible tempers, and these are just a few of the sick freaks I have had to deal with on a daily basis, and not all of them are inmates. There was a time where I almost lost control of myself after I was attacked by that psychopathic killer; for a moment, I was contemplating on killing him. In my mind, I came up with forty-one ways to kill a bunkie. That's not me; I don't think this way. I don't wish to hurt anyone, but that's what the walls had done to me. Prison negativity was weighing heavily on my mind, body, and spirit. It took some time, but I got over it, and with the help of God, I did not hurt myself or anyone else (amen).

Living in fear while trying to pay a debt to society, I would say, is a cruel and unusual punishment. No one should have to live in fear, period. This is America, is it not? I have secluded myself in my own mind, isolating myself from everyone, becoming a house mouse, a hermit. I live on my bunk or in a cage, only coming out when forced too. My mind was affected by solitude; I've develop antisocial personality. I hated to be around others, and when I did come out of my bubble to gather information for this book, I found myself overwhelmed with depression. It saddens me to the point of despair when thinking of all the lives being affected by what's going on in America's justice system. The more I communicated with others, the more I came to understand I was not alone. Please hear what I am saying—prison is not always the answer; there are alterative solutions. We just have to use the gift that God has given us, our minds!

I mentioned my bouts with depression, a battle that still affects my life to this day. If you or a loved one suffers from sadness, anxiety, or feelings of hopelessness, pessimism, guilt, worthlessness, helplessness, loss of interest, or pleasure in hobbies and activities that were once enjoyed; decreased energy, fatigue, being "slowed down;" difficulty concentrating, remembering, or making decisions; insomnia, early-morning awakening, or oversleeping; appetite and/or weight loss or overeating and weight gain; thoughts of harming self or others; restlessness; irritability; persistent physical symptoms that do not respond to treatment, such as headaches, digestive disorders, and chronic pain, please do not be afraid to say something, it could save their life. These systems may last for days or months at a time, sometimes going on for so long that they hardly become noticeable, as if it is the norm.

Depression is treatable with medication, counseling, and lifestyle changes. Depression is made worse with alcohol and drug use. It is important to get the proper help from a doctor, psychologist, psychiatrist, or anyone skilled in dealing with depression. Depression can kill if it goes untreated, it happens all the time in prisons throughout the United States. The sad truth is, dealing with depression while in prison, in most cases, is ignored, overlooked. Jail and prison facilities disregarded the symptoms and inmates that go untreated are released back into the community without professional help (it's cheaper that way). Your mental health is very important. Being in tune with your emotions and thinking patterns play an important role in your successful transition back into the community, and yet it gets overlooked and/or unnoticed because these scars are not visually displayed on one's face for all to see.

I live in constant fear because I am in prison. I am tired of being afraid, always looking over my shoulder, trying to watch my back. I am not OK; I am tired of being a human punching bag! All my years in prison has taken a toll on my physical well-being. I have developed numerous ailments that make my life very uncomfortable. I have a constant and displeasuring ringing in my left ear from having my head kicked in. I have seen my share of violence and physical abuse while in prison, and it has hurt me more than simply on a physical level. Being beaten and having your anus ripped apart by a man's penis is damaging both physically as well as mentally.

I had my finger broken because someone else felt they deserved the ring I was wearing, the wedding band my wife gave me. It was stolen right off my broken finger, and there was nothing I could do about it. That may have been harder than the rape, and trust me, even saying that is hard.

For those who have never slept a night in a jail or prison, a jail or prison mattress is like sleeping on a concrete floor with a wool postage stamp for a blanket (with no pillow). Now imagine sleeping like this year after year. Today's prisons conditions are worse than they were back in 1971. I live in chronic physical pain due to my incarceration. Throughout my incarceration I'm forced to sleep on paper thin mattresses, some were missing much of its stuffing. Some had mildew on them. More often than not, they were shorter than I was (I'm only 5'7" and most of the mattresses I've been given were much shorter than I). These conditions deprived me of sleep and, when sleep did come, forced me into positions only a contortionist could achieve. After all those years of sleeping on such a hard surface, I now suffer joint pains, lower back and hip pains, and neck and especially shoulder pain. Not to mention the constant headaches that I am sure are related to the listed ailments above.

I have also mentioned the inadequate amount of food given to inmates while incarcerated (yes, we know this is a problem), but it is the insufficient nutritional value in what is being served that is the bigger problem, especially for those like me, who has done a lot of time in prison. Year after year with an insufficient diet constitutes the very meaning of cruel and unusual punishment. When all you have available to eat are foods that are high in sodium, saturated fats, trans fats (hydrogenated unsaturated fatty acids), and cholesterol, one does not need to be a dietitian to know it is not a healthy diet to live on. And as I have mentioned in a previous chapter, the water here on prison row is so unhealthy that all prison staff are warned to bring their own. I can only wonder of the damage the water has done to my liver and kidneys.

Nevertheless, I can testify to feeling unusually weak and tired all the time. I have little energy, like my batteries are running low. I know this can be a symptom of depression, but I also know that due to the many years of not having a proper and balanced diet, I lack many of the essential vitamins a person needs to be healthy and to stay healthy. I am sure the unhealthy feelings I have contribute to the depression I suffer. Depression and the feeling of being unhealthy walk hand and hand. It is a vicious circle that plays havoc on my very existence.

My father-in-law is a retired food services supervisor (FSS) for the Idaho Department of Corrections. He worked the kitchens at a few prison throughout the state of Idaho. Food service managers (FSM) get bonuses for going under budget, keeping the cost of food down. Inmates who work in the kitchen get a ten-dollar bonus each month if they help keep the amount of food being served to the general population down (no wonder inmates are starving while in prison). All jails and prisons facilities have menus. These menus are a true deception, and that is fraud and corruption at the cost of the humanity. The food that is being served is not the same item that appears on the menu. For example, on the menu there is "meatloaf," and yet there is no meat in the meatloaf. A healthy diet is the building block of a healthy life.

In prison, you must be able to adapt and learn to cope with many uncomfortable, embarrassing situations—for instance, the act of being raped in prison. How we problem-solve and move forward from such nightmares can make or break any human. Physical health can have a profound impact on your transition from prison back to the community, and it is imperative to take care of one's self while behind walls. When you are tired, run down, and generally do not feel well, you are not inclined, in most cases, to take the necessary steps toward getting your life back on track. Managing your physical and mental health requires an awareness of life skills. It is not so funny. On one hand, they (prison dietitians, clinicians, and other officials) talk about eating right and how it will affect your transition back into society and then on the other hand, they give you a rotten piece of fruit to eat for lunch.

I have gone through some dark and very troublesome times during my incarceration. My mind and body have been put through the fire, my spirituality tested. There were times I lost all faith in my ability amid the pervasive gloom of my hopeless situation. There were times I worked myself into a mental frenzy, became deeply distraught and suicidal, banging my head against a wall (repeatedly) causing it to bleed, wanting to die. I had many thoughts of hanging myself (there was guy in the unit I was in who was selling rope by the foot for those who wanted to hang themselves). Realization, the awareness of where I was, only increased my depression. I was so obviously distraught, and yet no one seemed to notice or care enough to say anything or to do a thing to help. There were times I felt as if my spirit was broken. I would often play devil's advocate by questioning God's very existence, and yet I knew the inner conflict I was having with God wasn't me but the evil dwelling within me. Yet I questioned my faith, questioned God himself. I was in a hell; this metal anguish just fueled my hate, my hurt, my frustration. John Milton once wrote: "The mind is its own place; it can make a hell out of heaven, or a heaven out of hell." Of course Milton had never known the hell of prison.

Yes, I am traumatized by being beaten and raped while in prison. I still relive these nightmares most nights, and then I must survive it during the day. The aftereffects have been harder than the actual beatings and rape. I feel alone in this mental torture. The flashbacks of what I have experienced stop me in my tracks; it hinders and paralyzes my ability to move forward. I have lost all sense of humor; I have not smiled or laughed in what seems to be forever. I used to be a happy-go-lucky person; now that person is gone. Prison has taken away something that was good in me; at times it feels as if it has taken away all that is good in me. The ongoing trauma, relentlessly being victimized. No question, I have developed emotional and psychological problems. Prison has taken away more than just my freedom. It is killing all that is good in me, turning me into a state created monster, and I am left powerless in its wake.

Murder—it happens more often in prison than one might think, and often to more than just one's soul. Knowing I could be killed because some mental case is having a bad day is just a fact of life behind the walls. Unlike the real world outside the walls where respect is earned through actions and deeds, respect is something demanded behind the walls. Respect is everything in prison. The difference between respect in a county jail, and prison is that—if you disrespect someone in a jail, it could cost you a few teeth, a bruised eye, or a fat lip; you disrespect someone in prison, it could get you killed! Case in point, during my research, I have come to see how true evil takes its course, where one man kills over unpaid drug debts and gets away with it, over and over again.

Drug debts are taken very seriously behind the walls, and the situation I am about to tell you of is truly a diary of a madman. A young inmate sentenced to prison for the first time enters with a preconceived notion. He has the delusion that doing time is a badge of honor, that life behind the walls is a place where sides are taken, us against them, inmates against police. He has no idea that prison is really every man for himself.

He makes a few friends and falls into a drug crowd, the same type he would behind outside the walls. This poor delusional soul ends up supplying his friends with the expensive substances, with the promise that they would pay him back later. Of course his would-be friends had no intention of repaying him and all PC'd up (moved to protective custody) in some way (all intentionally did things to be taken to the hole and/or be moved away). This foolish young man ends up owing this maniac, a prison drug dealer a lot of money ($500).

This lunatic prison drug dealer wanted his money, but of course, this kid was relying on his friends and had none. Our young friend felt powerless. He was not accustomed to the goings-on behind the walls and knew not where to turn. Sexual acts were out of the question and he resorted to giving up his lunches and most of his other meals, he was starving himself. This was not good enough for the dirt bag he owed the money to; in fact, his every action was taken as a sign of disrespect and the cold-hearted drug dealer could not be disrespected. He could not allow others to see someone go without paying their debt.

It is no secret that HIV, the AIDS virus, is common among the homosexuals and IV drug users behind the walls. The prison drug dealer is friends with a pedophile, who also happens to be a customer and drug user who carries the AIDS virus in his blood. He gives his AIDS-infected customer a free sample in return for the syringe used to administer the drugs. He then loads the contaminated syringe and gives it to the young man that owes him the five hundred dollars, telling him it is a peace offering and that he wants the young man to start making transactions to pay off his debt. The young man jumps at the offer and unknowingly injects himself with the Aids virus. Not only is the drug dealer using this individual as a mule (someone that transports drugs), he also purposely infected him with a life-threatening disease and is killing him slowly.

The term *STD* is not specific for any one disease but represents more than twenty-five infections and organisms spread through sexual activity and the dozens of disease systems they cause. STDs are almost always spread from person to person by sexual contact, but some STDs such as Hepatitis B and C, virus infections, and HIV (AIDS) infections can also be spread by blood to blood contact, particularly contaminated needles. Pregnant women with infections may pass their infections before birth, during birth or through breastfeeding. Passing the HIV virus willingly and knowingly to another person is attempted murder, according to the law! Those two individuals who conspired, and in fact infected, that foolish kid with AIDS had just gotten away with attempted murder, though many throughout the prison knew of their conspiracy. Why did they get away with it? Because in order to survive behind the walls and not leave with AIDS or beaten to the point of brain damage, it is imperative for people like me to keep eyes, ears, and mouth shut. Make like the three monkeys—hear nothing, see nothing, and say nothing, and just keep walking.

I once believed that post-traumatic stress disorder (PTSD) was something made up, an excuse for an action that one could not accept. However, prison has changed that concept for me in a big way. I now know and accept the fact that PTSD is real. Invisible scars are no less painful or permanent than physical scars. I know because I carry them daily. The PTSD which I have come to know has manifested in the form of panic attacks, anxiety, nightmares, rage, paranoia, and hallucinations. I am in a constant state of loss of control. There is no question—I and many others like me suffer major psychological consequences from the hard and violent dysfunctional life behind walls of a prison. I have irreparable memory damage. I cannot sleep; my attitude changes from bitterness and despair at the drop of a hat. I hate people. I don't trust anyone any longer, and I do not want to be touched.

I feel tormented in my own punishment, a soul destroying torture that strips away my dignity. I am tired; I have no will. I feel less than human, shameful, unsubstantial, as if my very dignity has been stripped, my pride and confidence taken. I am emotionally depleted, mentally drained, and totally empty. I am tired of moving through this brilliant emptiness, the hell within my own head, with no end, with no hope in sight. My entire life feels as a hellish punishment. I am shell-shocked by what I have been through and seen, prison is death by a thousand cuts. And many good people leave prison with some form of PTSD.

As I receded further into the depths of depression; I survived only by the grace of God himself! It was my faith that helped me through my darkest hours. There are churches and chapels within prison. Knowing the only way I was going to make it through my time was to rely on God to guide and help me, I made my way to the prison chapel. I went to the house of God to find my sanity and found only another hell. The room next to where I went to pray was filled with devil worshipers, literally. Under the same roof of God was devil worshiping of all kinds. I was frustrated—how could this type of behavior be allowed under the same roof. Nonetheless, I would like to go on record that I'm in no way disrespecting or infringing on anyone beliefs to each their own.

Weeks later, feeling the need to speak to my God once again, I found myself entering the sanctuary. Relieved, I took a seat in a pew toward the back and began to pray. I was suddenly disturbed by two men at the other end of the pew and glanced over only to find one man stroking the other's penis under his coat. I had no idea that this is where the GBGs went to play with each other. I found out later that men were caught engaging in oral sex all the time behind the chapel. Needless to say, I will never go back. For now, I do my praying and talking to God on my bunk.

How does one focus after experiencing a traumatic event? Understanding what happens to one's mind, body, and spirit when exposed to trauma is vital to recovery. Knowing I am not alone, that there are many like me is crucial to moving forward. For now, keeping a close relationship with my lord and savior gets me through to the next day. However, the realization that I need to seek professional help haunts me, because try as I may, I am unable to find any within the walls.

CHAPTER 17

Family

M ore than half of America's 2.3 million prisoners have children under the age of eighteen. In other words, one of every twenty-eight children within the United States has an incarcerated parent. And half of those incarcerated parents were their child's primary financial provider before being incarcerated. It should be noted that according to the Brooking Institute, African-American parents who did not graduate from high school are 50 percent more likely to spend time behind walls before their child's fourteenth birthdays. With this being said, it is obvious that the most common victims of mass incarceration appear to be the family members and the children of those imprisoned.

The families of those incarcerated certainly do not benefit from their loved ones' prolonged incarceration and unemployment, and they suffer disproportionately high levels of poverty. The majority of these families are on some kind of assistance, welfare, or some other kind of government assistance at taxpayer expense. In other words, the taxpayers are not only paying for those incarcerated but the families of those incarcerated as well. And I will state this again so you can better grasp what it is I am telling you: it is the children who suffer the most from mass incarceration.

Millions of children never get a chance at a normal life due to mass incarceration within the United States. The truth is we know that children whose parents are actively involved in their lives do better in school than children who do not have parents around. They are less prone to depression, have better social skills, and are more likely to become good parents themselves. Parents are children's nurturers, teachers, and role models, and yet mass incarcerations are leaving these children behind and those in power act as if they do not care, that our children, our future, does not matter.

Children are emotionally healthier when they know they belong to a family. Children benefit by having family rituals and traditions. It is important because it helps tie families together in a positive way. Families with strong ties have the most traditions; these traditions provide stability in a child's life. Traditions are events that families do year after year, and it is a fact that such traditional events tie families together.

Helping children develop positive cultural identities is a tremendous gift, and a necessary one at that. Sadly in today's society, it is being ignored, overlooked (where are the family values?). No child should be left behind because of mass incarceration, especially incarceration for profit, and the new family traditions of doing time with a parent or a child is insane. It must be stopped.

Strengthening families today will help keep families together tomorrow. I am bringing to light this darkness of what mass incarceration is doing to American families and to our children, yours and mine. Destroying lives before they even get started is absolute madness!

During my prison stint, I have lost family members, my grandpa Norman (RIP), my aunt Terry (RIP), my uncle Rob (RIP), and a very special man to me, a great man, my uncle Gary. My uncle Gary is my mother's younger brother, he was always there in my life, no matter what. He was like a father to me. I remember that very day, the Fourth of July, my uncle's birthday. I was half blissfully and half longingly thinking of my family, imagining them together celebrating the two birthdays, my uncle's and our nation's, when I was called into the sergeant's office. I was told to call home, that there was a family emergency. The sergeant let me use the phone in her office, and I called my mom. I was relieved when hearing my mother's voice, knowing that she was all right, but sadness filled my soul when hearing that my uncle Gary had passed away from a heart attack.

I have dealt with death before, while in prison, but my uncle's death affected me very differently. It took a moment to get past the shock, for my brain to register what I had just been told. After my initial denial, anger set in, and then the hurt and sadness took over. Worst of all was the feelings reserved for myself. I cannot describe the emotional turmoil I struggle with, the not being there for my family (its eats me up in side). The shame of not being there for my mother, my aunt Gloria, and my cousin Jon.

Now, today, and every day for the rest of my life, I have to live with the fact that I was not able to show my respect and my support to my family by being at my uncle's funeral. This is not easy. I struggle with this shame and guilt, thinking maybe if I was out and not in prison, just maybe my uncle would be alive today. Men like my uncle are few and far in between. The world is a sadder and lonelier place without him.

The year 2016 was a very hard year for me while in prison, both mental and physical. My mother is and has been sick for many years, and in 2016, her sickness continued to get no better. My mother struggles to keep her diabetes under control. I am not sure what type she has, it being type 1 or 2, all I know is that she needs to use a needle. In the last few years, she has also had three strokes and a stent was placed somewhere near her heart area and recently, my mother has come to acquire vascular problem as well. Every time we talk on the phone, there is always something new going on and she never feels well. I have come to accept the fact that I may never see my mother again, never again meet her eyes. My mother has had cancer four times since I went to prison—once in the throat area and skin cancer three different times. The three strokes she has had have significantly slowed her down, and she has not been the same since the first one.

Somehow she continues to push on as new ailments continue to be—the latest is four blood clots, three blood clots in her stomach and one in her lung. My mother was hospitalized eight times last year

(2016) and went to the emergency room another nine times. When I asked how many times she went to a doctor's office last year, (2016) she said, "Sixty times would be on the low side." She has been prescribed twenty-two different kinds of medication. This is true madness because every new pill creates another new problem; this has become a vicious cycle just to stay alive.

I know my mother will not last much longer, and yes, I am scared to death. Knowing that if she passes while I am in prison, it will in no way be good for my well-being. The feeling of uselessness, of disappointment, and of not being there is the most disturbing part. I don't want my mother to die while I am in prison, knowing that I will not even be there for her funeral. The guilt of such thoughts is enough to break any man! I pray every day for my mom to hold on. The stress is the killer of my soul; I feel I am dying from within. I love my mother very much, and I was blessed to have her has my mom. Besides praying, I thank her every day. Every day, I count my blessings not just for my mother but for my father as well. I have been very blessed with both my parents and worry daily for their health.

The month I was denied parole for the fourth time, my father had a stroke. I come to understand and realize that neither of my parents may be alive when I get out of prison. I am very disturbed by this; fear constantly plays with my mind. I am truly afraid of sharing the same guilt, the same shame of my uncle's death, of the heavy burden on my shoulders, on my consciousness.

In November of 2016, I had to tell my family I would not be coming home—again. I have told my family this same story many times. I was on schedule to complete my assigned treatment programs in December and be home sometime in the middle of January 2017. However, the parole board denied my parole and told me to come back in a year without even a reason to why (though there is supposed to be transparency, few are ever told why).

It is no secret that in recent times Idaho's prisons system (parole board) has been cherry-picking the hard core inmates, inmates considered institutional problems and releasing them on parole back into the communities, keeping the more passive and easy-to-control inmates of nonviolent convictions with no major medical problems in prison for financial reasons. This policy and behavior by the parole board helps keeps prison cost down and the problem inmates out (though they usually come back to prison within the same year), therefore keeping the wheels of justice turning.

Before my first release from prison, I was given two difference release dates. The second time I got out, I was given six different release dates, three of them in the last month of being imprisoned. Even if you do have a date, more often than not, that date will be changed again and again. In Idaho, you have no idea when you are getting out, not until you are told that moment right before you walk out the door. The system does not allow you and your family to plan ahead and prepare for the future. Not knowing when I will ever go home is absolutely mind-boggling (without question, this is a form of mental torture on every inmate and their family, especially those who have children at home, who are waiting for their parents' return).

As I have mentioned before, I have been well-behaved, a model inmate for the prison system, and yet I have been denied parole four times. The stress of not knowing is overwhelming on my mental well-being, not to mention on my family's health, and yet this form of torture is legal and justified. Both my wife and I know we are at the mercy of others and have no future as of now. As I have stated before, my wife is legally blind, and for a few years now, she has been struggling with some serious pain in her hip area. The doctors say she needs a total hip replacement and she is waiting for me to get out of prison to have this surgery. It was not easy for me to tell her that I was not coming home in January, knowing that she was living in such pain and waiting for me to get home so I can be there and help in her recovery. Her pain was my pain. Today, I still have no idea when I will be home again, and I have yet to tell her that I must go to a halfway house, that I cannot come home. I have also failed to tell of the $450 in state extortion money for a halfway house I must come up with before I can get out of prison. How is this not extortion?

Half-way houses in Idaho may or may not be affiliated with the justice system. Idaho state officials do not require half-way facilities to be licensed and there are no codes or laws, no state, city or federal overseeing of these facilities. In fact, without state licensing, there is no way to know how many half-way houses are actually operating in Idaho. The last time I was extorted into going to a halfway house in Boise, Idaho, I shared a room no bigger than a closet with three other guys, guys who were always high on some kind of drug. Halfway houses in the Boise area are a scam, a rip-off; they do nothing for a person who has been released from prison. They take the transitional funding (the money) paid by the taxpayers, and once the funding (money) is no longer available the half-way house manager then kicks the individual out into the streets (like an unwanted dog) and those who get kicked out usually go on the run (skip out on their parole) because they are afraid of being violated and/or they become homeless before being sent back to prison.

Individuals on parole must immediately report to their parole officer about being removed from the halfway house. I have seen parole officers handle these situations in a couple of different ways. If your parole officer understands and is a decent human being, he or she may just tell you to go to a homeless shelter and will work with you, help you. And yet I have also seen the same situation, just different people involved go a different way. The parole officer violates them immediately, sending that person to jail for not obeying their conditions of parole. This is truly unfair, and it needs to be addressed. It effects many lives, creating more problems in the community without the public awareness. Halfway houses are not what you think or what they were intended to be. You should be concerned about what is really going on in these halfway homes in your neighborhood—trust me, it's not good!

From my own experience and everything I have come to know, nothing is done other than lip service that promotes and encourages keeping families together, nothing at all. What I mean by lip service is exactly what it means—it is all talk. There is nothing at all being done to help children stay connected with a parent who is in a jail or prison, especially here in Idaho. The system does not care if a family is connected or disconnected, unless you have the means (cash) to pay for the *services* provided by the jail or prison facility. All jails and prisons seem more than willing to take your money, profiting from your loved one's incarceration. Many families are being disconnected because they cannot afford to stay in contact and/or are not held in the same area they were convicted. There are no more face-to-face visits at county jails; all visits are conducted through the Internet, on a computer, or some other electronic device. Not all families have such means or luxuries to access the Internet and go without visual contact with their loved ones. Even if the possibility exists to do so, the family must pay a high price for video visits. How is this not extortion?

I went months and months without seeing my family because both my wife and mother did not know how to use a computer or any other electronic device to access the Internet. Not all people in this day and age are current in the use of new technology. No family should have to go that long without seeing each other, especially children!

Idaho's prison facilities still have face-to-face visits, and they are a privilege; this privilege is made very clear to all inmates and especially to all family and friends who come to visit a loved one in an Idaho prison. Prison staff members facilitating visits are, more often than not, mean, rude, and disrespectful to visitors. During one of my mother's visits, she and the other visitors were forced to wait outside in the cold while it was raining, until the front doors were opened, allowing visitors to enter. My mother was the first visitor in line when the front doors were opened, and as she was entering, she slipped and fell hard on a wet floor, breaking a bone in her hand.

Prison staff was well aware and witnessed my mother's fall but refused to help her off the ground even after medical staff arrived. What kind of people refuse to help an injured old woman off a wet floor? Moments before those front doors opened to allow visitors in, an inmate had mopped the area and didn't put up a "wet floor" sign. The worst thing about this was not the fall or breaking a bone in her hand—the worst thing was the lack of concern or respect the staff showed my mother after she fell. Is this the world we live in, a world where heartless souls working at a prison will not help a woman pushing seventy years old off the wet floor when she is hurt and in pain? Because of what my mother went through and how she was treated by prison staff, a lawsuit was filed, and in the end, the Idaho Department of Corrections settled out of court.

Though my wife's visiting story is different, it is every bit as disturbing. When it comes to mean, rude, and disrespectful behavior, Idaho prison staff has taken it up a notch by making my wife feel uncomfortable due to her disability, her vision impairment. This behavior is truly a form of discrimination, and it is heartless. I'm no way complaining in how IDOC operates its visiting operations. As I said, it is a privilege according to IDOC.

Nonetheless, I would like to say there have been many of times I have left from having a visit from either my mother or my wife with tears in my eyes, it is what it is when in prison.

But I will be honest not all my tears were from saying goodbye to my love one's. I have shed many tears from hearing the cries of a young child, crying out I want my daddy, come home daddy, come home. There's nothing sadder than seeing a mother drag a child out of the visiting area because they want their fathers. Again, I will say to you it's the children who suffer the most from mass incarceration for profit.

In a previous chapter, I briefly mentioned that during my last criminal case, the criminal charges and situation involving my wife, Michelle, that I had seven different public defenders (public pretenders). In the beginning of this nightmare, as I was waiting my turn to see the judge, I was escorted by a sheriff's deputy to a small conference room where my current public defender was waiting for me. We talked only a moment, no more than three or four minutes I would say. After our short talk, I was escorted back into the courtroom. I sat in that courtroom waiting my turn hour after hour and yet my name was not called. Court took an afternoon recess, and I was escorted back to the basement holding area. I was confused and uncertain to why I had not seen the judge, something felt wrong, I sat hour after hour in Ada County's cold wet basement until I was again escorted back to the courtroom. As I sat there waiting my turn, a gentleman I had never seen or talked to before called out my name. Surprised and wondering why this guy was calling out my name, I responded to his announcement.

As it turns out, the public defender I spoke with earlier that morning went home sick right after she and I had talked (she didn't look sick to me). This gentleman was now my new public defender. He filled me in on what happened and what was going to happen, none of which I truly understood. He left a few minutes later, and again I was waiting to see the judge. About a half hour later, I was pulled out of the court room by a sheriff's deputy and placed into a side area off from the courtroom then escorted into a small conference room. I had no idea what was going on, and again I felt that something was wrong, not right. As I sat and waited, I started to panic and worry. The longer I waited, the worse I felt. It seemed to be forever, but in true time, it was not more than ten minutes before my new public defender came into the conference room and said, "There is a problem."

While my new public defender was outside the court room waiting for court to reopen, a woman who he had represented many years before recognized him and started a conversation with him. Just my luck this woman was my wife Michelle, there's the problem. And since my new public defender was once her public defender, this was a problem. Because he had represented my wife years ago, this was—and is—a conflict, and he had no choice but to excuse himself as my public defender. I was shocked, but there was nothing I could have said or done, and my hopes of seeing a judge that day were over.

A month later, I was back in court with another public defender, the fifth one. My public defender asked the court for continence because he was not prepared. Another month went by before I was back in court with another new public defender, the sixth one, and again my public defender asked the court for a continuance. I never had the same public defender more than a month and only talked to all of them for maybe a total of half hour at the most. Between court dates, my sixth public defender came to the Ada county jail and we had a talk. It was understood what we were going to do concerning my case. I liked my new public defender, and she was the first one to come and talk with me at the jail. Up to that point, I had never seen or talked with a public defender other than a moment right before I went in front of a judge.

So again I was back in court, sitting on a hard bench in a cold courtroom waiting my turn in front of a judge. As I was waiting, I see my public defender walk into the courtroom. She walked to a back corner and sat down, going about her business. Court was back in session. Finally, my name was called. The prosecuting attorney stood and addressed the court, saying my lawyer was not present and asked the judge for a later call, telling the court that my lawyer should be present at a later call. I was just sitting there watching all this, not saying a word, but saying to myself, *My lawyer is right there, and yet she's ignoring my name when being called. Why isn't she responding?*

An hour or so later, my name was once again called, and again my public defender was still in the corner not responding to my name. This time I stood up and said, "My public defender is right there." By standing up, I got every one's attention, not good. I was hauled out of the courtroom violently and pushed so hard into a holding cell I fell to the ground. Because my hands were in restraints, shackled to my waist, I fell hitting my head on the concrete floor (good times). Shortly after, I was then escorted back to the Ada county jail without ever fully understanding what happened.

The next day, I called the public defender's office in Boise. I was told there was a problem and the public defender's office would no longer assist in my defense, with that being said, they hung the phone up on me. I just stood there with the phone to my ear, listing to the disconnected beeping, wondering what to do.

Weeks later, still having no idea of what was going on, I was pulled out of my cage and told I had a visitor. It was late, ten-thirty at night and this was something that was far from being normal at the Ada county jail. I was escorted to the old visiting area where I met guy behind a glass wall. He asked if I was James. I answered as I sat down. He introduced himself and stated that he was my new attorney. This guy was now the seventh public defender on this one case (he was a conflict attorney who handled conflicts between defendants like me and the public defender's office). As it turned out, that fourth public defender who had represented my wife many years back was a conflict to my current case. At this time I was told he need time to go over the file and have an investigator talk with my wife and mother.

By the time I had been appointed this attorney (my seventh), I was starting not to care anymore. I just wanted it over. I was willing to do anything to make the nightmare end. The system had beaten me down physical and emotionally. I was tired of telling my story over and over again to people who didn't care. It didn't feel real anymore—it became a story in my head, and every time I told it, I became conflicted. Was it the truth or make-believe? I was in a constant state of confusion. I was truly mentally and physically beaten. I would have admitted to murder just to get the hell out of my head. With each new public defender, they all became a false prophet, and this conflict attorney was no different. At first he listened; they all did at first. He assured me that he had my back, or so he stated. He talked a good talk, but that was it. His actions, his behavior, were far the worse than all the other public defenders I had combined.

As my case moved forward, my court-appointed conflict attorney asked the courts for continence after continence all at the expense of the taxpayer. Months later, things just did not seem right to me, so I asked my court-ordered attorney what was going on. Turns out, the district attorney's office had not sent him my file and he was still waiting for it, or so he said. I was devastated when he told me he had not read my file. Weeks of torment passed before, again, late at night, I was pulled out of my cage. This time my attorney informed me he had gotten my file and that he had talked to prosecuting attorney handling my case (this was the same prosecuting attorney who handled my first case). As our conversation continued, the subject changed, he began to tell me what the prosecuting attorney had said about my wife, Michelle.

I sat silently for what seemed forever as he went on and on belittling Michelle, my marriage, and my family. He exceeded the words of the prosecutor and began speaking of the character of my wife, how bad she was for lying to the police. He went on explaining that she had a history of lying, that she had serious character defects and that he believed her to be mentally ill. "Sick in the head" are the words he used, words that still echo in my mind. As I sat there listing to my own attorney telling how horrible of person my wife was, I tried to tell myself that the words he was using were of the prosecuting attorney prosecuting my case.

I am not sure how long this went on, the world spinning around me seemed to be in slow motion as I took in what I had just been told. There was a sudden moment of awkward silence in which neither of us could meet the eyes of the other. He shuffled some papers and kind of cleared his throat, then says, "Your wife is very cute in a childish way."

"That's enough!" I yelled out slamming my hands on the table as my chair went crashing behind me. "Who the hell are you to be talking about my wife like this? You don't know her, you don't know me!" I took the next few moments to gather my thoughts, as I paced around my fallen chair, and then once I realized what I needed to do, I look him right in the eyes and said, your fired.

My conflict attorney was not there at my next court appearance. However, there was another attorney from the same office. This fill-in attorney told me that my lawyer went on vacation and he would be back in two weeks. I told him I had fired that SOB and that I never wanted to see him again. I am not a confrontational type of person, and am usually sheepish in matters such as these. But I knew for a fact that this fill-in attorney knew of my firing of his associate, leaving neither of us knowing what to do next (I'm sure his firm had already billed the courts).

I don't remember what was said next, but it was understood that my fill-in attorney was to represent me in court that day and that he was going to ask for another continuance. I cannot find the words to explain how hard it was for me to accept yet another continuance, but I could not allow this private firm appointed by the courts to bully me. Besides, he was there to ask for an extension anyway. The continuance was asked for, and the court granted the request. This fill-in attorney was technically my eighth representing me on this one case (I was told this was a normal procedure in Ada county).

I had not seen or talked with anyone representing me in weeks and was totally clueless of what to expect. At the time I didn't know who or how to notify anyone for legal help. It was a matter of minutes before my next court appearance that I was once again escorted to the very same conference room where I found the very same conflict attorney I had fired weeks before. I was shocked beyond words as I sat across from him but had a lot I wanted to say. He began speaking as if nothing had happened between us, as if I had never fired him. County jail has a way of playing on one's mind, disrupting one's thought process and often leaving one unsure of what is happening, as if living in a totally separate reality. My mind was worped totally gone I was hungry and tired, at this point I just wanted this madness over even if I had no clue what the hell I was doing.

My attorney began explaining that he and prosecuting attorney had discussed my case over dinner, and between the two of them, my future was laid out. The deal was, take the deal or get a life sentence. Those were the terms. On top of that, they threatened my wife and mother with contempt of court among other charges, sealing my fate. When I went to sentencing I was forced by my attorney and by the prosecuting attorney who was prosecuting this case to lie, to admit to a crime I did not do. I felt I had no choice my family was being threatened.

Michelle was fifty-two years old when she and I were married. She was a disable veteran and had obviously lived a life long before we were married. Her past was her past, and I had no concern with it, and no one else should either—our marriage was no one's business but ours. I had waited twenty-two years to find a woman like her, a companion like my wife, and I was not going to throw it away because of a mistake. Our marriage was far from perfect—then again, what marriage is? A good marriage is about more than attraction or even love. A good marriage is about forgiveness and compromise; it takes work and that is not always easy. We, as humans, are not perfect, we all make mistakes. But I truly believe that God is on our side, that there is a higher power watching our backs. And I know that God brought me and Michelle together, blessing us with so much of his love that it spills over into ours. At the end of the day, we learn from our mistakes. We apologize to one another and move forward, together, no matter what.

My point is that it is not just me in prison—my family, Michelle, was sentenced with me. We both had a part, and we were both sentenced to prison—mine is just more physical than hers. However, though we are both yoked with this burden, it is her who has saved our marriage and I respect that because I don't believe in divorces. When I married Michelle, I married for life. I take the words "Until death do you part" literally. Not a week passes that my beautiful wife does not come to the prison to visit. I am so grateful for her love. I thank God before and after every visit and ask that he keeps his hand on her. Love conquers all, even prison. Idaho has taken my freedom, but it can't take the love that my wife and I share.

I live every day knowing Michelle struggles to survive, that I am not there to help, that I cannot do my part as a husband. My wife's visual impairment creates a lot of stress for me, so much so that I think it is source of the frequent nosebleeds I have been suffering from (this happens approximately five days of the week). My wife needs assistance to do the everyday, normal things that most people take for granted, like cooking without burning down the house (which almost happened once) or walking without tripping over something (this is why my wife needs a hip replacement). I have to believe that God uses situations like theses to bring families together. After nearly burning down the kitchen, God put it on my Uncle Gary's heart to help. He replaced the damaged stove with a brand new stainless glass top and he had it installed for my wife. He was there for me and Michelle when I couldn't be.

Communication is the key to any relationship. I am not simply talking about speaking to one another but true interaction. However, in order to communicate, one must have the ability to speak to one another. When I was first arrested, my wife immediately put money in my inmate account so I would be able to make phone calls (no one can make a phone call from a jail or a prison if they do not have funds on their account to do so). Once there are funds on your inmate account, then and only then is it possible to place a phone call outside of the jail or prison. But not all phone calls are possible simply because there is money in your account. The person you want to call must accept the phone call on their end before any communication is allowed between the two parties. This allows the person called the opportunity to accept or to refuse the phone call being made.

My wife and I talked a lot over the first weekend of my arrest (all phones are recorded in all jails and prisons). When I went to video court Monday morning, a no-contact order was put in place without my wife's permission or knowledge. After video court, I called my mother and asked her to let Michelle know that I was no longer able to call due to this court order. Days later, I received a letter from Michelle asking to please call her as soon as possible. She also wrote that the no-contact order was just that—*no contact*—and that it did not stop us from talking on the phone.

She was scared; everything that I had taken care of was now on her shoulders. I was warned by other inmates that my wife's assumption was wrong, but I had learned that the inmates were usually wrong in their advice and that you can get any answer you want if you ask around enough. I tried to contact my court-ordered attorney (my public pretender) but found that an impossibility and decided to call home. Besides the fact that I loved and missed my wife, she had verbally let me know (through her letter) that she wanted to speak with me, and I couldn't say no.

When I called home (a total of seven times), it was Michelle who not only accepted but paid for the phone calls. Our conversation had nothing to do about my case or why I was in jail, they were personal and about business, about bills and other things Michelle needed to know. As I said, she was worried; we both were. I was virtually yanked from her life, and anyone that loses a spouse will tell you that even the little things can be overwhelming. Everything I took care of was now on her hands.

I am years past my parole eligibility date, sitting in prison not knowing if I will see my mother or father again. I doubt that I will see my grandfather, who is ninety and very sick. He and I are very close; I am the oldest grandchild on both sides of my family. My grandpa, Paul, is a good man. I miss him very much and worry every day that he will pass while I am in prison, that I will have to live with the regret of not being there for him, for my family, and for myself. And then there is my father-in-law, Laszio, who is ninety years old. A man who escaped Communist-ruled Hungary back in the 1950s while under gunfire in a small airplane. His actions, his bravery has given me a love for freedom

I carry to this day, even while imprisoned. He is a big part of my life, and I pray he holds on until I get out. Laszio loves his daughter, my wife, very much. My wife is very lucky to have a loving father who has always been there for her. Yes, family is very important and it should not be taken for granted. Life is so fragile, so short. And because I put myself in prison, much of the important things in life have been taken away from me. I miss birthdays, holidays, and deaths and have lost contact with most of my family because of my imprisonment.

I have exposed myself to you, explained in detail about many embarrassing situations that I have had to deal with since coming to prison, so this should be of no surprise. There has not been a night since coming to prison that I have not cried myself to asleep. I cry for my family, my wife, mother, and my children. Though I weep for my children, I know I never have to worry for them. God gave me good, intelligent kids; he has truly blessed me in this way. My oldest daughter practices law in the Los Angeles area. My youngest daughter is a veteran (US Army) who served in Afghanistan during her military career. I have grandkids now. Unfortunately, I have been in prison so long I have yet to see them face-to-face, to hug them and to love them as a grandfather should. With these few words, I would like to apologize to my family for not being the man, the father, the grandfather, the person my parents raised me to be. I am truly sorry.

I have lost a lot of time over the years, been away from my loved ones way to long, and that's on me. I'm the one who is responsible for being disconnected. However, the sad truth is that I cannot afford to stay connected while in prison; it's just too expensive, and that's on the system.

Six months after writing this chapter "Family" my worst fear came true on May 30th 2017 at 11:00 a.m., my mother Sandy Kay Kühnel passed away from colon cancer she was sixty-eight years young.

And sadly on December 12th 2017 my grandpa Paul passed away as well. As I end this note I would like to tell my mother, "Mom, I will forever keep that promise" and thank you for being my mother. My world has gotten a whole lot smaller and a whole lot sadder.

CHAPTER 18

Change

For those incarcerated in a United States jail or prison, the amount of effort to help promote change and right living within those institutions is next to none. Prison is not about helping people better themselves through positive change, but about human warehousing for the profit of a few. Profit reserved strictly for wealthy corporations and individuals believing they are above not only the law but the very taxpayers they are reaping these huge benefits from. That's right, I am saying you are being ripped off, and the cost is in more than your hard-earned dollars but that of human lives.

Mass incarceration is the biggest scam in American history, and we all should be upset about it. The time is now—start questioning the motivations behind mass incarceration. Question why your tax dollars are ending up in the pockets of wealthy corporations who, in return, lobby for stricter application of laws and harsher punishments. Question why your money is being wasted warehousing minor drug offenders for years then releasing them back into the community with a lowered self-esteem and outlook on life than when they went in. Individuals are leaving institutions worse off than when they went in, many having no idea of how to change or the willingness to do so.

Redemption is possible, people can change, but unfortunately, mass incarceration will not allow it. Ex-cons are doomed by their criminal past and reminded of their mistakes daily. Constitutional rights are stripped and they are forced to mark convicted felon boxes on job applications, leaving many feeling condemned forever. Many can never outlive their past; it is held against them long after they had paid their debt to society. When will the past stop becoming the future?

Change starts with education; it starts by understanding that change is needed and long overdue. Change starts with accountability, holding our leaderships to a higher level. Changing the way we think and operate will, in return, bring change. No one can force change; it must be taught. Change must be made believable, people must be guided and shown a better way. We the people must have the attitude, the commitment toward excellence. Millions of lives and families across our nation are at risk, and failure is not an option. We must promote change in our justice system and in our jails and prisons. The future of America depend on it.

Obviously, I need to change my thinking and how I behave, and I have admitted my shortcomings. I have expressed my forgiveness to my lord and savior. Change starts within and then moves outwards. Change starts with providing those who want to change, the tools and opportunity to make that change. People who are in prison need help and assistance; they need to see that change is possible and obtainable. Therefore, when leaving prison, people are better prepared and equipped to make the changes needed in their lives. People want change; they just need the help to make that change. How can anyone improve their well-being if there is no help available while incarcerated? How can anyone improve their well-being if there is no help available after they leave prison? Where are the health care, social services, education, and the jobs for people like me who get out of prison? I have yet to find any useful help here in Idaho. I wonder why there is no help here in Idaho for those in Idaho. People need these types of services because they have been raped, beaten, and robbed by a system that taught inmates this is what inmates do to one another while in a prison. As of now, our prison system teaches one to become less moral and helpful to others, creating hardened criminals for life. This insanity must stop today!

Idaho has very few resources to help ex-cons with the transition back in to society. I have applied for them all and have also been turned down for all. I was told I did not qualify, that my inmate account had shown too much activity while incarcerated and/or there was no funding, no money available. Where is all the money going? Recovery from prison is a process; it takes help to regain one's self-worth and, in many cases, mental stability, and few ex-cons are able to redefine themselves without that help (this is a proven fact). I have heard it argued by the hard-core right that the imprisoned deserve nothing from the public for breaking the law. That tax dollars should be spent on schools and other needed things rather than wasted on criminals. Statements such as these allow one to dodge the real issue. I am not saying that education should not be a priority, but why shouldn't it be just as great inside a prison? Why should one mistake define a person's entire life? A majority of inmates will be released and returning home to neighborhoods like yours. Would it not be better for all if those inmates were prepared through education and job training to move forward rather than return to the same rut that placed them in prison? If you expect people to change when released from prison, then offer then help, real help, because real change takes help.

I have yet to find any help inside a prison that was useful. When released the first time, I was forced to participate in a program, just because my parole officer said so. It had no value in helping me at all, simply something intended to keep me busy. I was extorted for thirty dollars a week on top of restitution and cost of supervision. In fact, I was paying a hundred and eighty dollars a month just to stay out of prison, getting nothing in return for my money other than hardship. And this does not take into account the cost of transportation and other underlying costs involved with simply attending classes and maintaining contact with parole officers. This was not helpful especially when every dollar counts. I went without food and was paying my bills late because I didn't want to go back to prison.

If you are a veteran, behavioral health services may be available at the Veterans Affairs Hospital (VA) in your area. The VA offers dozens of support and therapy groups. They also offer social groups, problem-solving classes, focus groups, transgender (LGBT) support groups, PTSD groups, mindfulness-based stress reduction, and many other kinds of recovery groups. It is truly amazing what is available if you are a veteran. My wife is a veteran, and because of her being a veteran, I am able to participate in some of these programs. Upon my release, whenever that may be, my wife and I will be taking advantage of this great opportunity and better our lives with positive change.

The first time I was released, I had nothing. Everything I owned had been stolen by my ex-girlfriend, and there was nothing I could do about it. When I got out of prison, I was forced to stay in Idaho, I tried to apply for a transfer to go home, but Idaho would not allow it. I was forced to live in a place I had never lived before. In order to survive, I had to borrow money from my grandpa the first month I was out, my first days out and already in debt, not a good start (it is what it is). Now that I am a felon, finding a job was not so easy. I applied for dozens of jobs the first month out. Before prison, I was a certified auto technician; I had been my entire adult life. It is all I knew, it was who I was, and I was proud of what I had accomplished and learned throughout my career. Unfortunately, my ex-girlfriend stole my livelihood by stealing my tools; she stole in the neighborhood of forty thousand dollars in tools, and the messed-up thing is that I am still paying for them, tools I no longer have. Because I went to prison, I lost everything. I have come to realize I have no career without my tools. Everything I have worked for and learned was gone and useless all because I went to prison. Starting over when you are almost fifty is not easily done.

I was a train wreck when I got out of prison. The shame and embarrassment of being raped began to haunt me. I told no one. I hid it from my family. I tried to contain it within, box it up as if it had never happened (bad idea). As I pretended it didn't happen, I tried to move forward in my life. I finally got a job (minimum wage). I went back to school at a local college. Within the year, I had all my debts paid up-to-date, but no matter what I was doing, the nightmares continued on and I was having trouble sleeping and eating. The guilt the shame of what I went through while I was in prison was catching up with me. I turned to drugs for help, and I would be lying if I said they did not help, at first.

I was spiraling into a hell within my own head. Then a miracle happened. I meet a women. It had been so long since I had companionship and someone to talk with; it was nice to have someone to just say hi to at the end of the day. When I meet Michele, our relationship was nothing more than being friends. Having Michele as a friend was a life-changer. I lost the desire for drugs and started to feel better about myself; I wasn't so lonely anymore.

For one to change there must be willingness and help available. I needed help when I got out of prison. Unfortunately, there was no help available for people like me, people who suffer from a traumatic event while in prison. The state of Idaho does not recognize this as being a problem and offers no help. From my own experience, I believe it would be in the best interest of Idaho and its citizens to give people who leave prison the help needed to better themselves. States that mass incarcerate their citizens for profit need to be more reasonable, aware to what mass incarceration does to a mind, body, and spirit. It is only right that these states offer help, such as behavioral health groups and workshops that help people cope with being raped, beaten, and robbed while in custody in a state prison facility, for free. Professionals who can help people like me, like psychiatrists, psychologists, social workers, mental health counselors, peer support specialists, and most of all, trauma symptom management, should be available to everyone leaving a prison.

If I had gotten professional help immediately after my first release, just maybe I would not have come back to prison. Many people are suffering from PTSD, and there is no help when they leave prison (hospitals do not send sick people home without their meds). If I would have been in tune with what I went through and what happens to the mind, body, and spirit when exposed to trauma, I would have done more to help myself. But because of the embarrassment, the shame of it all, I pretended it did not happen, fooling myself that it was just a bad dream. I ignored the truth, and now I am back in prison.

I have come a long way, but it has been an unbelievably slow process in which even admittances was hard to accept. I now fully accept my responsibility of failing to help myself. Helping me is also helping others who are in the same boat as me. First we must admit our shortcomings, our wrongdoings, and then we must forgive ourselves and move on by getting the help that we need and want one step at a time. Life is too short; it's time to live and breathe free.

My only motivation is to help bring change, to educate all about mass incarceration for profit, and to inform how seriously this situation has become. Mass incarceration really began in the seventies as a way to curb voting rights of those considered undesirable (African-Americans, hippies, and the poor white population). And then it took a radical turn when it was discovered that there were huge profits to be made from this human suffering, exploding legislation of new laws and mandatory sentencing, in return exploding prison populations.

As I have stated before, jails and prisons are needed. However, the problem is that our justice system has mutated because of money, greed, and the power involved. What is justice when it is based on how much money can be made? Justice is becoming what is affordable in America. Our prisons are not full of the wealthy. A Wall Street banker defrauds millions of Americans on their home loans. Though fraud is a criminal charge, not one wealthy banker was held accountable in the 2008 housing market crash in which millions of Americans lost their homes due to illegal marketing strategies. But a man selling loose cigarettes on the streets of New York is choked to death on camera for avoiding sales tax. And that is exactly what American justice has come to. I believe it is time to make a change. I truly feel our forefathers would not agree to what going on in today's courtrooms. There is selfishness rather than selflessness.

Again, my motivation is to help myself by helping others. I have an obligation to tell my story because my story is an American story shared by many. Until now, I have not shared to anyone—no one, not even my wife—about me being raped, beaten and robbed, while I was in prison. I am exposing myself to you, to the world, so the truth can be known. This is my story, but it is not about simply telling my story. This book is about saving American lives, especially the children, by exposing the truth about mass incarceration for profit. We as Americans have the power to stop this American tragedy, and now that you know the truth, you can make a difference. The life you save just may be someone you know or love. Please contact your local senator or congressman and address your concerns about mass incarceration for profit, today.

Sadly, on December 14th 2017, I went back in front of the Idaho commission of pardons and parole for another parole hearing. The parole board was aware of the book I was writing and it was obvious by their tone they did not approve.

At this time, I was denied parole for exercising my constitutional rights specifically the first amendment, freedom of speech, and I was resentenced to another sixteen months in prison. Though I was upset with their decision, I was not surprise. I was warned by an IDOC education instructor; this person warned me that the parole board will see my book as a threat. And I was also warned by the women who conducted my preboard hearing interview back on October 10, 2017. And I was warned by one of my treatment program facilitators.

All three warned me, they all tried to discourage me telling me that I was wasting my time that writing a book will do no good, and it will jeopardize my chance for parole. Obviously, I did not take their advice because I truly believe that my freedom and my life are not as important as the truth. The truth at all cost must be said, it must be exposed no matter what even if it cost me my freedom, my life, and possible, my marriage.

Idaho/IDOC and the Idaho commission of pardons and parole are hoarding inmates, it's a proven fact. For example, I've been eligible for parole since July 9, 2014, but I'm not the only one being held in an Idaho prison years past their parole eligibility date. What I'm saying is there are thousands of Idaho inmates who are eligible for parole today who have completed their assigned treatment program who are being denied parole time after time. Idaho is refusing to release its inmates when there fix amount of time has been served and because of this Idaho prisons are max out full beyond their capacity.

In December 2017, it was announced by late spring 2018 Idaho will be sending inmates to a private prison in another state. This is Idaho answer to its prison overcrowding problem by sending Idaho inmates out of state to do their time.

Long story short, Idaho is going back in business with another private prison to house Idaho inmates out of Idaho.

Truth is, if Idaho released those inmates who are eligible for parole today this alone would reduce the prison population tremendously. And it would save tax dollars and most of all not a single Idaho inmate would need to leave the state of Idaho to do their time. Idaho's politicians don't want the public its citizens to know that they are hoarding inmates for profit at their expense.

And I predict at some point, Idaho's elected public servants will use the media to manipulate Idaho citizens into thinking that Idaho needs to spend more money to accommodate for the prison over-crowding problem. I'm saying it right now none of this is necessary, but it will happen at Idaho's tax payers expense.

While other states are revising their sentencing guidelines and re-ducing their prison population, Idaho on the other hand is doing the complete opposite. It's prison population has sky-rocketed, growing approximately six percent annually for many years. Even if Idaho built new prison facility in 2019, it would not help or solve Idaho's prison over-crowding problem, what so ever. Idaho would have to build a new prison facility every four to five years to accomodate for its prison growth. Regardless, even if Idaho built a new prison facililty today, who are they going to hire to staff their prison?

As of now (2018) all Idaho prison facilities are under-staffed, meaning the Idaho Department of Corrections can't find enough bodies to fill all job vacancies they currently have now. Much less staff an entire new facility. Reason being; IDOC does not pay enough, shifts are long and brutal. Truth is who wants to work in a hostile, life threating work environment for peanuts (un-less of course you happen to be an elephant). And need I say, who wants to deal with A-holes all day long, no-body wants that!!

With that being said, I would like to share with you an un-spoken side-effect that comes with the job of being a correctional officer.

Sadly correctional officers, they them selves, more often than not, are effected in a negative way, while working in a hostile and life threating work environment. They them selves, can and do become a product of their environment (in this case a product of their work environment). They them selves take that negativity and all the bull-shit home with them, thus becoming A-holes them selves. Unfortunately it's the nature of the beast when working in a correctional institution. This un-spoken side-effect not only effects correctional officers, but their loved ones as well, resulting in a high rate of divorces and suicide among correctional officers.

Idaho is at the forefront of human warehousing for profit, and its corruption is state-approved, state-facilitated, and administratively encouraged. Idaho has always pushed the boundaries of constitutionally acceptable punishments. It is a system that treats you better if you are rich and guilty than if you are poor and innocent. Race, poverty, inadequate legal assistance, and prosecutorial indifference have all collided to create a textbook example of injustice. We are on a brink of a new future by ending mass incarceration for profit, and it starts now!

Words on paper by themselves do not change the world. I am saying, we the people need to reexamine the system as a whole. Mass incarceration is built on lies. Perhaps knowing the truth will allow us to begin to return justice to our criminal injustice system. To fight injustice, we must rise together. Some of the most important changes happen where they can't be seen—in your mind, in your heart. And I pray that your doubts and many questions have grown too ripe to ignore. The truth is only a few keys away. All you have to do is Google it. Mass Incarceration for profit is not something we as Americans should not be proud of.

CHAPTER 19

The Conclusion

Since the completion of this book *Carceration State: A Struggle to Live Beyond Mistakes*, I have come to realize if I truly want to help in the cause by bringing awareness to mass incarceration for profit and help those who can't speak for themselves. Then, I must continue on writing and never stop informing, reporting, and exposing unjust, corrupting, and abusive behavior by those who control our American justice system and institutions.

With that being said, there will be another book, "Oh yea," I plan to follow up with another book called: Carceration State Vol 2: A Struggle to Freedom in the near future.

Sadly, our American justice system to our courts, jails, and prison institutions have lost their meaning of what they were intended to be. Justice and due process has become an afterthought second to the greed of a dollar.

And because of this greed, too many good citizens in our great country are being exploited for profit.

Truth is, being poor in today's America, you will see a different type of justice. And because you don't have the money for an adequate defense, you will have a slim chance in receiving a fair just sentence. And again, I will say today's American justice system is a system that treats you better if you are rich and guilty than if you are poor and innocent. This is not justice for all, its favoritism based on the size of one's pocket book.

Today's America has a prison population of 2.3 million, and there is another half million or so more locked up in county jails waiting for their day in court at any given time.

And there is approximately 7.2 million or so Americans who is under some sort of correctional supervision at any given time. And might I add another disturbing fact, the United States incarcerates more juveniles than any other industrialized nation in the world. Our American justice system are locking up men and women and its children at an alarming rate, discriminating against African Americans and Hispanics much more than those who are white. There are tens of millions convicted felons living in the United States today, I believe this merits America's attention your attention.

As I have already mention, jails and prisons are needed in today's world, and their walls and cells should be reserved for the worst of the worst kinds of people in our society. We, as a nation need to rethink our approach to crime and punishment.

Our American justice system should be focused on just punishments, accountability, the truth, and justice for all. Unfortunately, due to greed and power our justice system is being run as a business putting money ahead of justice and lives.

Before I went to prison, my belief was if a person who was in prison they must have done something really bad to deserve to be there, sadly, that's not the case. And because of our public servants' abuse of power for profit, felony convictions mark men and women for life. Being a felon in today's America, almost guarantees poverty to the individual and to their family. Our American justice system is being used as a fundamental weapon of repression and for profit. America has commercialized incarceration by turning it into a business. Today's mass-incarceration (for profit) has gotten so out of control, prisoners (our brothers and sisters) are no longer recognized or treated as human beings. They are property, a product for profit.

And because of this, this makes mass incarceration the most pressing civil rights issue of our era. America is a nation based on human rights isn't not? When constitutional rights are being violated and or ignored, I believe every American should be concerned. Why because their rights are your rights, and if it can happen to them, who's to say one day it won't happen to you? This is why I'm writing what I'm writing because once our rights becomes a privilege, none of us are safe.

Obviously, I'm not a professional or even a decent writer. I'm just a dumb-ass who is struggling to live beyond mistakes. Nonetheless, I'm doing my best to bring attention to this abuse of authority that's destroying our great country while locked in a cage. Regardless of my writing ability, my goal is to make sure that what happened to me does not happen to you or to your son or daughter, or anyone else. No one should experience what I went through while paying their debt to society.

I have many goals and one of them is to bring awareness, to alert the American people of this growing problem and give them the opportunity to correct the problem. For our great country, for humanity, we must change the process of how we treat our fellow Americans. I pray you will change your views and become understanding of this growing problem. And help in the process by bringing a positive change in our justice system in the way of reform (nothing will change if nothing changes). Truth is, I need your help, America needs your help, and together we can bring changes by making a difference that will save lives and tax dollars.

This change starts with being proactive in your community. Americans needs to ask questions by questioning everything that is going on in their communities. Ask yourself are the elected public servants in your area doing the job taxpayer's are paying them to do. You have a right to know whether your public servants are performing their duties competently and most of all ethically. The only way to fight injustice and corruption is to be proactive in your community. And by holding those accountable for their disservice to your community.

Although this is my story, and yet it is the same sad story which too many Americans have in common. President George W. Bush in an annual state of the union message said that people in prison should return to society better than when they went in. Sadly, this is not the case. America's moral compass is all messed up because of greed and power. Mass incarceration is built on lies, perhaps knowing the truth allow us the opportunity to return justice to our criminal justice system.

I wish that I could end this sad story with a happy ending, unfortunately, due to greed, I'm sorry to report back in February 2018, Idaho announced they are sending 250 inmates to a private prison facility operated by the GEO group in Karnes City, Texas. Sadly, I must report the majority of these inmates left Idaho kicking and screaming not wanting to leave. My heart is filled with sorrow for these inmates are being isolated even further away from their loved ones. Idaho is planning to send additional 750 Idaho inmates to private prison out of state in the months to follow.

Concurrently, as of 2018, Idaho is doing business with two different private prison corporations to house Idaho inmates. The newest one GEO group and the other is Management and Training Corporation (MTC). MTC runs the CAPP facility within Idaho's prison row community. The CAPP facility is one of the smallest prison facilities in Idaho, and it is one of the most violent ones as well. There are many reasons why the CAPP facility has so many problems and a high rate of violence, most of it comes from the lack of respect from the warden, of course, poor quality of food, and poor living conditions are also a contributing factor as well.

MTC and the GEO group are in business for profit, reducing recidivism would be bad for their business. Idaho tax dollars are being wasted by private prisons whose business to house human beings not to reform, or to rehabilitate by helping those who are in their care. Private prisons cut corners to generate profits by understaffing its facilities providing inadequate health care, and lower employee qualification, (reduced training), substandard facility maintenance, and provides inmate with inferior food. The private prison industry generates billions of dollars in annual revenues and employs teams of lobbyists to persuade government officials to continue mass incarceration policies. Many Idaho politicians have financial relationships with private prisons. When elected public servants/politicians accept money from the private prison industry it brings the question to who's best interest they have yours, mine, or are they doing them and their job that best serves them and their pocket book.

When states like Idaho use private prisons to warehouse human beings it allows the state to profit at taxpayer's expense, here's how. A state charges its taxpayers' X amount of dollars per year per inmate. And when this same state uses walls and cells of a private prison facility, it can pay a private prison far less than what the state received and charged its taxpayers. This is one of many examples of mass incarceration for profit.

Idaho does in fact have a hoarding problem. Idaho does in fact have issues with corruption. And I truly believe, Idaho would not have a prison overcrowding problem if it didn't have issues with corruption. As long as corruption has control in Idaho, Idaho will always be a carceration state.

But there is a silver lining to this problem, if Idaho, today put an end to its hoarding, it would solve the Idaho prison overcrowding problem tomorrow. And I guarantee once the hoarding issue is resolved it will save millions of tax dollars each month. On the plus side, this savings then could be used to better educate Idaho's future—its children.

In conclusion, now that the cat is out of the bag, meaning this book, and what I have said especially about Idaho. I'm truly in fear for my life, so if I end up dead in a prison cell or found dead in a ditch once released from prison I assure you it was no accident.

To be continued and God bless, America . . .

ABOUT THE AUTHOR

James and Michelle Kühnel

James Kühnel was born in Germany in 1970. In 1977, his family moved to Simi Valley California. In 1993, James moved to Minnesota where he became an auto and light truck technician. In 2009, on his way back to Minnesota from California, Mr. Kühnel stopped off in Idaho to see his sick mother. Sadly, the rest is history.

CPSIA information can be obtained
at www.ICGtesting.com
Printed in the USA
FSHW011814040219
55447FS